APPLIED GRAPHOLOGY

APPLIED GRAPHOLOGY

A Textbook on Character Analysis From Handwriting

For the Practical Use of the Expert, the Student, and Layman Arranged in Form for Ready Reference To which is added an Appendix Containing a Complete Compilation of the Qualifications, Traits, Habits, and Propensities of Individuals, and Definitions and Graphological Interpretations

Illustrated with over 300 specimens

by

ALBERT J. SMITH

Graphologist

GYAN

Published by

GYAN

Gyan Publishing House
5, Ansari Road
Daryaganj, New Delhi-110002
Phone: 011-47034999, 9811692060
E-mail: books@gyanbooks.com

Distribution Network
gyanbooks.com
India, USA, Canada, UK, Australia, France

ISBN : 978-81-212-6002-2 (PB)
First Published, 1920

2nd Impression 2021

Printed at: Gyan Press, Delhi.

Applied Graphology
Author: Albert J. Smith

APPLIED GRAPHOLOGY

A Textbook on Character Analysis From Handwriting

For the Practical Use of the Expert, the Student, and the Layman
Arranged in Form for Ready Reference

To which is added an Appendix containing a Complete Compilation of the Qualifications, Traits, Habits, and Propensities of Individuals, with Definitions and Graphological Interpretations

Illustrated with over 300 Specimens

By

ALBERT J. SMITH

Graphologist

TABLE OF CONTENTS

PART II

PREFACE

"The French scholar Lemaire, once said, in discussing the possibilities of graphology: "It is a profound mistake to suppose that everything has been discovered; it is the same as to consider the horizon to be the boundary of the world."

When I began analyzing character from handwriting more than twenty years ago, I had to contend with cases where clients questioned the correctness of my analyses. A careful investigation convinced me that the erroneous conclusions were based on an incorrect understanding of the terms used to express the shade of meaning intended. Had these critics acquired a better knowledge of definitions, their criticisms would have been unnecessary.

These experiences inspired me to write this book.

All graphologists aim to use definite terms to express the shade of meaning intended, fitting generic or denotative expressions to the particular requirement of the case.

The skilled graphologist, with a keen understanding of definitions, will write his delineations in cheerful and pleasing terms, and will avoid all stinging references, to soothe sensitive minds, even though they may be justified. The analyst who adheres to the truism: "to be interesting, one must tell the truth audaciously," may find it more expedient to be less frank, if he would retain the good will of sensitive clients.

This book has been written with especial consideration for the student and the business executive. The manner of expression is left optional with those who prefer a modification of terms, without detracting from its effective purpose.

The habits, traits, and qualifications listed in the appendix, have been carefully selected to meet every demand. For each there is a corresponding graphological sign. The definitions that accompany these terms are authoritative and express the proper shade of meaning, from a graphological standpoint.

Unlike most books written on this subject, this volume is little more than a handbook or a textbook, with simple rules and data that define and explain the science of graphology, its relation to the mental processes, and the existing phenomena of handwriting by which one who has become adept may form a fairly correct estimate of the character, propensities, and proclivities of individuals, whose aptitudes, tastes, and talents are revealed.

No attempt is made to convert any one to its principles. The investigations of scholars for over four hundred years are sufficient evidence to sustain its claims. The dependability of Graphology rests on its skillful use and proper application. Its reliability as an index to character is indisputable, for

> "It is not so much what society believes about it,
> as what society knows about it."

INTRODUCTION

A person who is able to write, unconsciously performs this function without realizing the mental and physical effort required to form the letters or characters which were taught him at school. It is a manual operation performed spontaneously, without regard for the complex processes of mind, muscle, and nerve force involved.

A person's handwriting is really a part of himself; it becomes a habit, a second nature. This is why individuals are, and have to be, *themselves* when they write. Handwriting serves as a means for the expression of thought. It is the outward manifestation of one's personality, and it is fully as characteristic as one's manner of walking or tone of voice.

Investigation and experience have demonstrated that not one person in one hundred thousand writes the same style of hand he was taught at school, five years after leaving school. The reason for this modification of style is that after leaving school the individual assumes responsibilities that change his mode of thinking, which in the course of his adopted vocation make it necessary for him to write hastily with total disregard for the tutored style he was taught at school. In a short time he drifts away from his school hand entirely, and unconsciously begins to write in a manner best suited to his convenience. With the development of business training, this variance of style becomes fixed, as long as his individuality remains unchanged.

All features in handwriting are interpretable. Each reflects some trait or quality. As every one has a unique personality, so also, does he write differently from every other. This suggests the reason why there are no two handwritings exactly alike. Handwriting forms an intimate revelation of the inner processes of mental attitudes and emotions; in a word, it constitutes the expression of one's personality and moods.

Nature in her wisdom has endowed man with intelligence that enables him to give expression to his impulses and emotions, according to his individuality. These variations of mind-impulses provide the individual with the means for expressing likes and dislikes, which eventually form habits. These habits make character. And thus it is, that by exhibiting these various emotions in a greater or less intensity, individual temperaments are reflected in handwriting.

Style of handwriting changes with age. A man at fifty may not write the same hand that he did at twenty or thirty years of age, and should he live to be eighty or ninety, his chirography would in all probability show further indications of change. These modifications in the script will indicate that changes in the impulses and emotions have occurred.

No one can successfully disguise his handwriting. When an attempt is made to change the style of writing, the slope is the first thought that suggests itself as a means for shielding identity. Should the normal hand slope to the right, the most likely variation will be to write "backhanded," on the theory that this slant is the remotest in appearance from the natural hand. This change from the right hand to the backhand may deceive the uninformed; it may alter certain unimportant features in the writing; but it cannot deceive the expert, because the graphological features have not been affected, leaving the tell-tale markings. The appearance of the writing may have changed—due to the slant of the strokes, but the analysis will reveal the same characteristics in the writing, whether written with design or to rest the muscles of the hand, thus enabling the graphologist to detect the sham. Every natural movement of the hand has been recorded, making futile the effort to veil the identity of the writer.

Change of pens will not alter the distinguishing characteristics of handwriting, any more than a change of attire will change the personality of the writer. Every one instinctively choses a style of pen that best suits his convenience in writing, and this adopted style of pen enables one to write in a manner most natural and with less effort.

The skill of the graphologist is determined by his ability to neutralize the signs; the purpose being to *estimate* the strength or weakness of a sign. This balance of "credits" will determine a fixed habit from one that is occasionally displayed.

The student should make himself familiar with the elements of graphology, in order that he may gain a knowledge of the basic principles of the science. Study and commit to memory the rules, without which no successful results are possible. At the beginning the student will meet with many different specimens of handwriting, some of which will show conflicting signs. If proper weight is given to each sign, by deductive measures any conflicting sign may be overcome.

Before any attempt is made to interpret the character of others, the student should practice with specimens of his own handwriting, analyzing and delineating from them until he is able to check up every phase of his character from the script. Advancement may be tried with the handwriting of intimate friends, conducting it in the same manner as with your own. Further advancement should be tried with the handwritings of casual acquaintances, checking up those traits known to you, and trying to verify those that are not at once apparent, by association or inquiry. But whatever you do, remember that no one but yourself is deceived should you undertake to discount your shortcomings or exaggerate your good qualities.

The student should be careful to select the proper word to express the meaning intended. If you mean *accuracy*, do not use the word *precision*. Consult the appendix for the definition of the word you wish to use; this will give you the shade of meaning. Do not credit a person with being *religious* when you should have declared that the writer was *spiritually inclined*. There are no known signs that would imply *religiousness* unless it be one of the characteristics of disconnected letters in writing. Use judgment and common sense, and stick to the rules. With practice, one may soon become a careful enough analyst for all practical purposes.

RULES FOR THE STUDENT

Examination of thousands of specimens of handwriting in all languages, by masters and students of graphology, support the conviction that there are no two handwritings exactly alike. In fact, no two agree any more than two personalities have the same potential qualities, or two facial expressions are alike. There may seem to be similarities, but on recourse to an analysis, the similarity is effaced.

These rules should be carefully committed to memory, as on a thorough understanding of them depends the accuracy of a delineation. The rule that applies to "neutralizing" the signs, is the graphologist's standard.

RULE No. 1. Some handwritings show practically no character, for the reason that the character of the writers is quite elementary. No more can be deduced from this kind of specimen than the specimen reveals, and the student must confine himself to what he finds and make no pretense to enlarge upon it, or to be influenced by deductions.

RULE No. 2. An ideal specimen for analysis is one written in black ink, on unruled paper, and containing not less than five lines. Although much can be often interpreted from a single line, it is always best to get all the writing of the person available.

RULE No. 3. An envelope is not satisfactory for analysis, as it is usually addressed with some degree of care. The inscription is therefore not spontaneous, and does not show as many signs, nor show them as truthfully as a written page.

RULE No. 4. The finest delineations are made by combining characteristics, and this is imperative if the work is to be accurate. The rule is: If two traits seem to oppose each other find their relative strength and from it deduce the resultant characteristic.

RULE NO. 5. Never read the subject matter of a specimen before making the analysis; at the beginning, the student will be tempted to do so, and may find it difficult to avoid. The tendency is to defeat the purpose and is likely to bias the judgment or adherence to rule.

RULE NO. 6. Left-handed persons do not write "backhanded" simply because they are left-handed. Most left-handed persons can use either hand, and write a forward style of chirography with one hand as well as with the other; this upsets the general belief that left-handed writers pen the backhand because they are left-handed.

RULE NO. 7. Distinguished men and women frequently write *very bad hands*. All professional men and women write *bad hands*. The greater the intelligence of a writer, the easier it is to interpret the writing.

RULE NO. 8. The most difficult specimen of handwriting to analyze, is that of the *illiterate* writer. This rule is nearly akin to Rule 1. Unless the features are clearly indicated and analyzable, it is recommended to limit the delineation to the merest generalities, using the most marked characteristics in the script, or else decline it for analysis altogether.

RULE NO. 9. A sign occasionally displayed indicates an occasional trait, and must not be elaborated upon.

RULE NO. 10. Any sign in a specimen may be strong or weak, plentiful or scarce.

RULE NO. 11. If a letter is given for analysis, the writing on the last page will be the most natural.

RULE NO. 12. A sign displayed occasionally, but strongly marked, indicates an occasional trait that is evident when aroused

RULE NO. 13. A sign frequently displayed indicates that it is a regular trait of the writer. When the sign is frequently displayed and strongly marked, it indicates a strong habit, and may be made the subject of positive assurance.

RULE NO. 14. There is no definite rule by which the chirography of the sexes can be distinguished, because there is no sex in mind.

However, it is usually not difficult to distinguish the sex in handwriting, for the writing of women is characteristic, as a rule, and is generally recognizable. Modern business training has given to women the masculine dash in handwriting, and may deceive the student as to the sex. The only advantage in knowing the sex of the writer, is that it enables the student to give more definite details, with certain modifications for the significations of the features according to whether they apply to a man or woman. Should it become necessary to know the sex of the writer, this information should be frankly asked for at the time of taking the specimen for analysis.

RULE No. 15. The student should provide himself with a small magnifying glass for examining individual strokes and dots.

THE ELEMENTS OF GRAPHOLOGY

These are the basic elements of handwriting, briefly defined for the convenience of the student, that he may determine at a glance the general significations as an aid to ready analysis.

The size of writing	Signifies details
The slope of writing	Attends the affections
The lines of writing	Denote the spirits
The shape of writing	Determines the intellect
The thickness of the stroke	Relates to the senses
The spacing of words and lines	Determines the breadth of mind
The speed of writing	Is indicative of the energy
The finals in words	Determine the degree of generosity
The capital letters	Measure the individual's taste and pride
The punctuation marks	Relate to the amount of attention, care, and culture
Signatures	These are the individuals' mark of importance
Flourishes	Indicate superficiality
Connected letters	Denote logical reasoning
Disconnected letters	Denote intuition
Down strokes that are firm	Signify will power
Down strokes that are weak	Signify weak will
Down strokes that are lightly made	Denote spirituality
Down strokes that are heavy	Indicate masterfulness
Down strokes that are *muddy*	Sensuality, materialism
Tops of small letters that are sharp	Keen perception
Tops of small letters that are round	Dull perception
When base line is irregular	Adaptability
When base line is even	Mental balance
When base line is wavy	Hypocrisy

FEATURES AND TERMS USED IN HANDWRITING WITH THEIR SIGNIFICATIONS

The graphological terms and their indications that appear under this caption have been compiled under two classifications, the *General* and the *Special Features* of handwriting. They are repeatedly used throughout this work and should be well understood by the student. The *General Features* of handwriting include the rudimentary or basic principles of writing, which alone are not competent for analysis! The *Special Features* refer to those elements that are interpretable, and to which the General Features are subordinate.

The *General Features* of handwriting include: style, size, form, slope, spacing, lines, strokes, and speed. The *Special Features* include: the down strokes, cross strokes, loops, margins, terminals, hooks, and the small letters. The capitals, figures, punctuation, and signatures are contributing factors, having significance only when associated with a written specimen; the signature, however, is interpretable when spontaneously written. Signatures are not always reliable material for analysis, apart from the text.

THE GENERAL FEATURES

STYLE

Style of handwriting relates specifically to the formation of the letters and the manner of placing them on the lines. It considers the general appearance of the writing, and has no connection with the signs and their analogous traits. Under this classification, are included three forms of writing, the *angular*, the *round*, and *the combination of these two styles*. As a matter of fact the several features that follow this classification, are, in a greater or less degree, expressions of styles to which this section is subordinate. No one writes the angular hand from choice; neither is the round hand chosen; they are habitual manifestations of individualities, the same as lisping or stuttering. A man writes the angular hand because his activities of mind and nerve force direct the strokes spontaneously; this is equally true of the round hand. The combination hand is a modification of the nerve functions, which induce a more tranquil hand. The angular hand is never written slowly. The round hand, when penned fully round, is never written rapidly, but the combination hand may be hastily or slowly written.

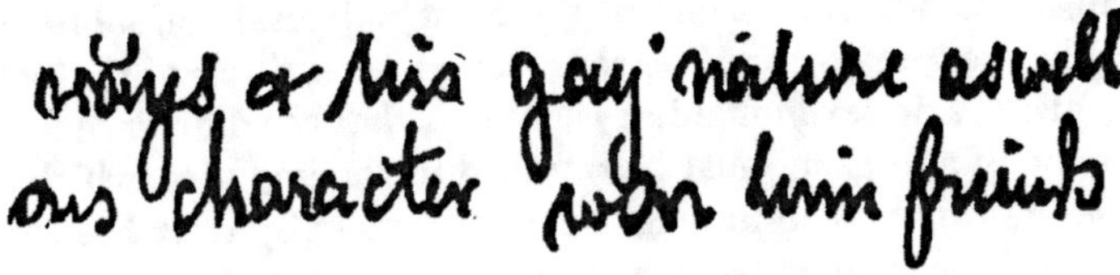

ANGULAR WRITING

This style of writing consists of sharply formed strokes with the tops and base of each letter pointed.

Denotes activity; nervous, quick, and energetic disposition. Mental alertness and physical restlessness.

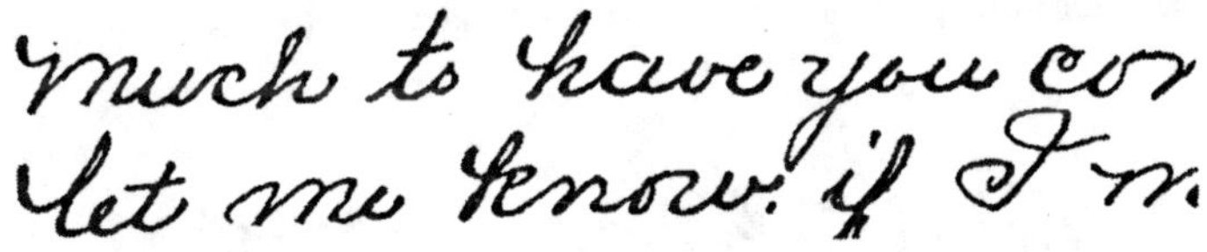

ROUND WRITING

The top, and occasionally the base, of each letter is rounded, not pointed. When the tops of the small letters are pointed, and the base is rounded, the writing is *abducent*, having nearly the same value as the angular hand.

Denotes constructiveness and order; tastes denoted are mechanical with strength, deliberation, clearness of conception, good judgment, coolness, steadiness, thoughtfulness, and a practical, patient, and resolute character exhibited.

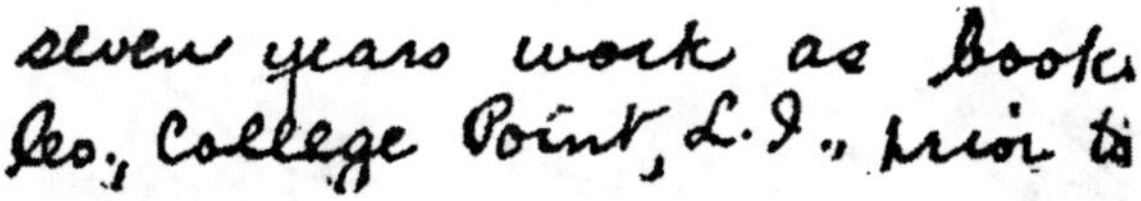

COMBINATION WRITING

The angular hand, tending to the round, and vice-versa.

Not naturally industrious; loves peace, rest, and enjoyment. Nature more or less passive. Little power of resistance.

THE SLOPE

The slope of handwriting has reference to the declination of the down strokes. There are three forms of slope: the *right slope*, that has to do almost entirely with the affections; the *vertical*, that marks an indifference to affection; the *backhand*, which in a certain sense, is a modification of the vertical hand, and always indicates cold heartedness. In judging the extent of the slope, the sex of a writer should be ascertained, for what might be considered as an excessive slope in a man's writing might not be so regarded in a woman's. As affection is one of the most universal traits of character, the great majority of persons slope their writing to the right, and as there is no sex in mind, it is obvious that the difference in the expression of affection, must be revealed in the impulses, which are stronger in women than in men. Men live more by their head and less by their heart than women, and these variations of impulse are evident in handwriting. The student is warned not to judge the backhand writer too hastily, as certain modifications of this style of handwriting are taught in libraries for use in indexing and labeling. This librarian style is easily distinguishable from the spontaneously-written backhand, and must not be confused with it.

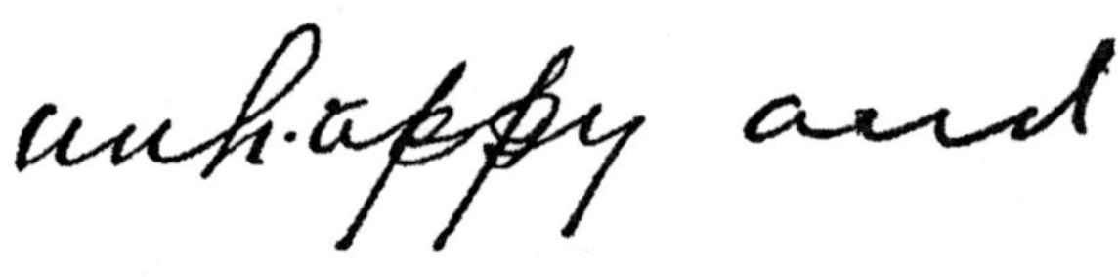

THE FORWARD SLOPE

The normal slope in writing is about 70 degrees to the right. This is the usual slope in all scripts of the Teuton and Roman forms of writing.

(*a*) A personality in which the emotions, feelings and sympathies govern. (*b*) Always susceptible to sentiment and largely guided by the impulses. Amenable to the common influences of life.

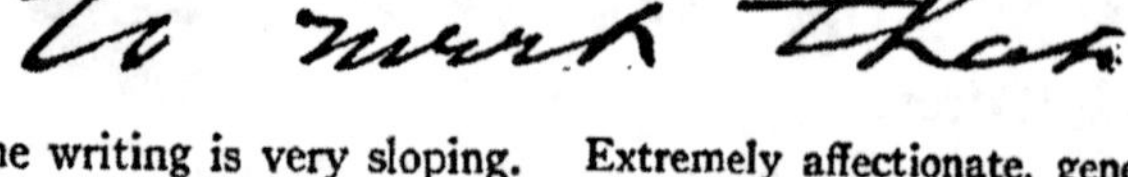

When the writing is very sloping.

Extremely affectionate, generous, and self-sacrificing. Inclined to be impulsive, animated, and demonstrative.

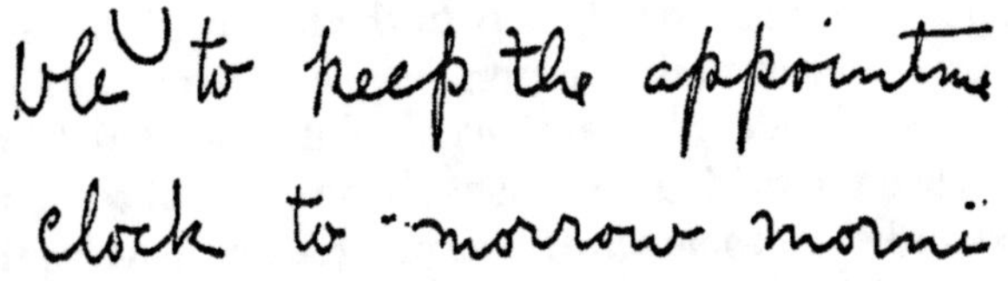

Vertical Writing

The upright or perpendicular stroke.

(*a*) Judgment and reason enter into all motives and actions. Whatever is done is tempered with self-restraint and deliberation. (*b*) Slow to move; does not arrive at decisions hastily; does not like to be hurried. (*c*) Generally determined and obstinate. (*d*) Sincere, constant, and loyal.

Backhand Writing

When all the strokes slant to the left. (This classification excludes the librarian's backhand, which is arbitrary and used for indexing and labeling.)

(*a*) Reason and self-interest are the governing motives. Natural reasoner and schemer. Self-conscious nature. Seldom does things impulsively; thinks first of the consequences. (*b*) Indicates ability in some direction; originality and self-reliance. (*c*) Not charitably inclined. (*d*) Little regard for authority; aptitude for executive and administrative work. Good leader—poor follower. (*e*) Generally quiet and reserved nature; does not become enthusiastic or excited. (*f*) Inclined to be artful and insincere; statements are not always to be taken seriously. (*g*) If other signs agree, a suspicious nature.

THE SIZE OF WRITING

The Size of writing ranges all the way from the almost microscopical to the inordinately exaggerated script of the egotist. About one-eighth of an inch in height is considered the natural size of writing. There are three sizes of writing: The *small*, the *medium*, and the *large*. What is meant by *small* refers to the height of the letters, as the wideness or narrowness of letters have a different signification, and are discussed under the captions of "Diffused" and "Crowded" writings. When the writing is very small, the power of concentration is indicated, although some script is so microscopical in size that it is almost unreadable, and this smallness indicates stinginess, particularly so if the words are close together. Medium sized writing is the customary size, and to gain any intelligent deductions from it, one must look to the other signs for the explanation of the script, for, alone, this size has very little meaning, no more than one would expect from any ordinary person of commonplace intelligence. Large writing, or high letters, approximating one-quarter inch in height, signifies the synthetical rather than the analytical mind. When the letters of large writing are all of the same height it denotes the opposite to large writing with all the letters at different heights. The size of writing must be judged carefully, as the value of it depends on the contributing signs. That the size of writing is not alone dependable for analysis, is explained by the fact that some writers accommodate their writing to the size of the sheet of paper used, while others, whose faculties are well balanced, are not influenced by any limited space.

SMALL WRITING

When habitually written low, one-sixteenth of an inch in height or less, excluding the capitals.

The general indication for small writing is the power of concentration. It betokens strong individuality and force of character, with mental powers above the average. Good thinkers and reasoners, with well-trained faculties. Literary persons, scholars, statesmen, philosophers, and men of mental refinement write small. (No one of mediocre ability ever writes the small hand.) Executive and business qualities with diplomatic tendencies are indicated.

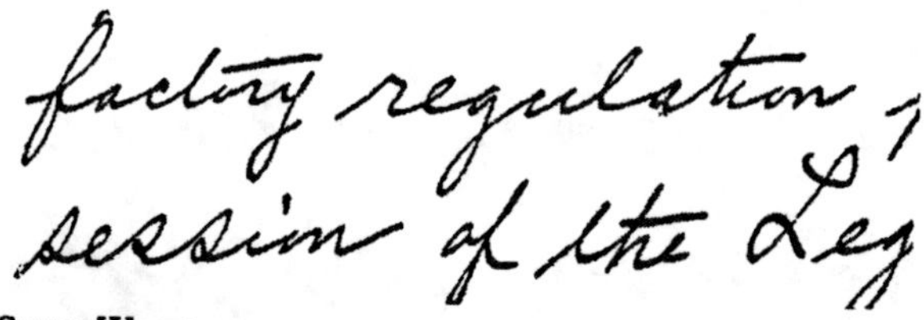

MEDIUM SIZED WRITING

The conventional hand; approximates one-eighth of an inch in height. Note: Consider the proximity of the writing to either the large or small script, and then neutralize the two extremes.

Not always concentrative; more of the physical than of the mental type. May have good thinking qualities but are poor reasoners. Not always tactful, unless the signs for tact are evident. May have some intellectual powers and originality, but they are not strongly indicated. Tendency is to the practical, material affairs of life. The signification for "medium" writing, depends on its proximity to the small or large script.

LARGE WRITING

This style of writing has graphological signification only when the small letters are abnormally high. (Follow same rule here as that given for medium writing.)

(The writer of this specimen is prominently in the public eye, and at one time was a candidate for the presidency.)

(*a*) Slight powers of concentration; thoughts are diffused and fly from one subject to another. Finds it difficult to remain long at one task; naturally restless and unsettled disposition. (*b*) The nature is one hard to satisfy. (*c*) Nature is close to the surface and easily seen, for the writer is inclined to be too outspoken, frank, and talkative. (*d*) Little tact is indicated; reserve force is limited. (*e*) Expends energy too freely and extravagantly in pursuit of fantastical ideas, and is apt to be too free in spending money, expressing opinions, in charities, or in use of words and ideas. Usually conscientious and of highest integrity, but lacking sound judgment.

When the writing is large and with flourishes and deliberate shading.

Denotes an egotistical, pompous nature, and given to boasting.

When writing is abnormally large and in the angular hand.

(The writer of this specimen is a woman member of the English nobility, and the wife of a member of parliament.)

Denotes order, zeal, and enthusiasm. Readily animated or excited. Always vivacious and spirited. Usually entertaining talker; insists on having own way whether it suits others or not.

THE STROKE

All handwritings are formed by combinations of the down strokes, the upstrokes, and the cross strokes. The down and cross strokes alone have any graphological significance. No one can write one intelligible syllable with the upstrokes exclusively. Down strokes may be written heavy, fine, or shaded. Heavy strokes may be made all one thickness or shaded, irrespective of style of pen used. Fine strokes are devoid of shading. Shaded strokes vary according to the amount of pressure put on the pen—one form of pressure determines the *position* of the shading on the down stroke, and the other form, the strength of the shading. Shading may begin at the top of the letter and end lightly; or it may occur midway down the stroke or at its terminal at the bottom of the stroke, before returning for the *upstroke*. An upstroke may be partially shaded at its

(This is a specimen of the handwriting of the late Miss Mollie Fancher, written in 1884, shortly after emerging from a thirty-day trance, in which she believed her spirit or soul was celestially transported to heaven, and was in commune with the angels.)

ners; little desire for voluptuous pleasures or luxuries of life. Usually spiritually inclined, although not necessarily religious. Always has a high sense of honor and kindly consideration for others.

SHADED WRITING

There are two forms of shaded writing, the *conscious* and the *unconscious* or natural shading. Conscious shading may be distinguished from the unconscious form, by noting the deliberate heavy down strokes, or inflated parts of the stroke, which are made to beautify the writing, or for effect. *Unconscious shading:*

Denotes an insistent nature; the more natural and spontaneous the shading, the more the trait is intensified. Natural executive ability always indicated, with determination. A distinctive personality with well-defined tastes. Fondness for physical pleasures, wholesome sport, luxury, and good living.

Conscious shading, done for effect.

Affectation and egotism with commonplace personality. Lack of culture and ability, with small education, and weak intellect. Lack of strength of character. (Young children just out of school, consciously shade their writing for effect; this feature is not considered in this definition.)

Shaded writing that is *Muddy*, unclean, coarsely made, with inflated shading; refer to *Heavy Writing*; see *Muddy Writing*.

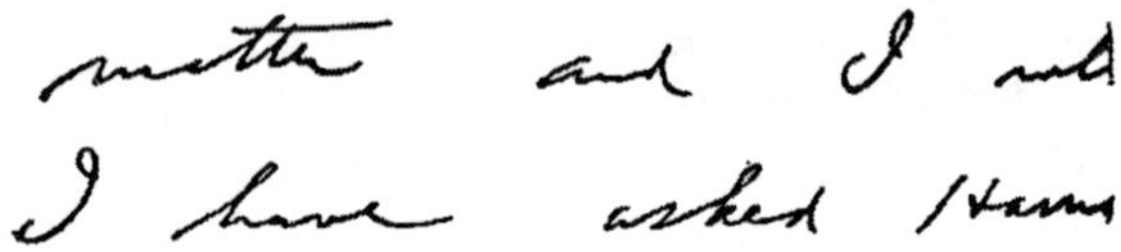

CROSS STROKES

When the strokes are light, no shade. — Denotes absence of sensuousness.

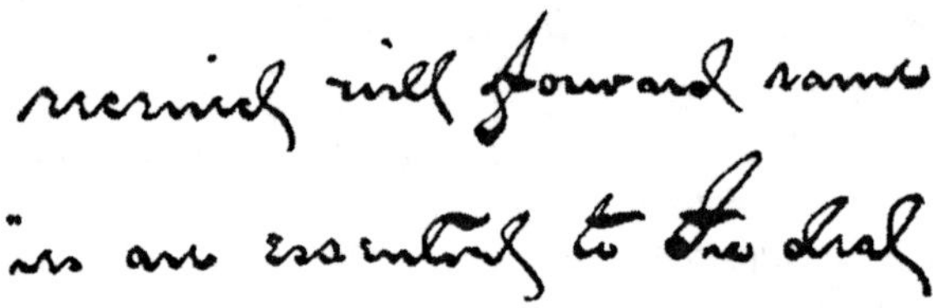

When the cross strokes are heavy and sharply shaded. — Denotes sensuousness with regard to form, music, or any of the emotions that are aroused by the passions.

FORM

The *form* of writing is closely akin to *style* of writing, with the exception that in style reference is made to a fixed standard conformation that is recognizable as distinct from other styles of writing. *Form* relates to the individual letters, the curves, strokes, and other characteristics in writing. Hence, the *copperplate* form is not typical; it is unusual as a means for conventional letter writing. It apes the Spencerian penmanship, and if persisted in, stamps the writer as of light mentality. *Conventional writing* is formal, expressionless, and may lack one or more of the elements that give character to writing. It is that form of writing that results from custom, habit, or preference, due to lack of mental force. *Inartistic writing* may indicate shallowness of intellect, or a brilliant eccentricity. The laborious scrawl of the hard working mechanic may appear inartistic, compared with the practiced hand of the experienced writer, but the intellect in either case may be equally acute.

Copperplate Form of Writing

The *copybook* style, written, with full regard for appearances, to beautify the writing; Spencerian penmanship. Not typical of normal handwriting.

The more the handwriting approaches the copybook standard, the more commonplace is the personality of the writer. Denotes lack of individuality, bound by rules and conventionalities; no ideas of one's own; no distinctive character. Accomplishments, ideas, and capacities are limited; seldom brilliant. Many bookkeepers affect this style in the belief that the tidiness of their books requires it.

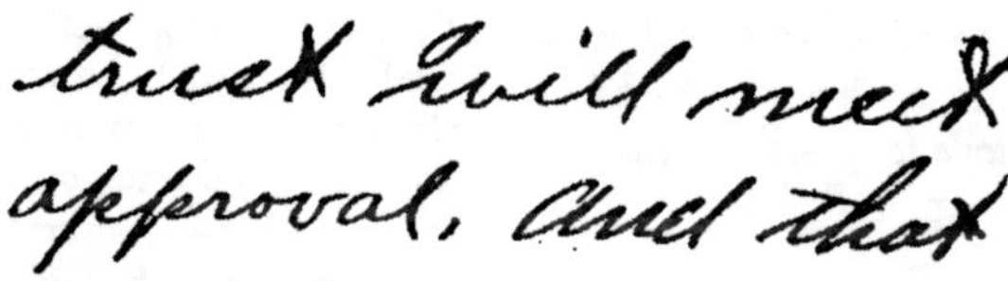

Conventional Writing

Unassuming, unaffected script, penned freely and without regard for appearances; the formal hand

There is no graphological significance to this style of writing; the only excuse for introducing it here is for comparison with the copperplate style and the inartistic. The separate features in the specimen will determine the character of the writer.

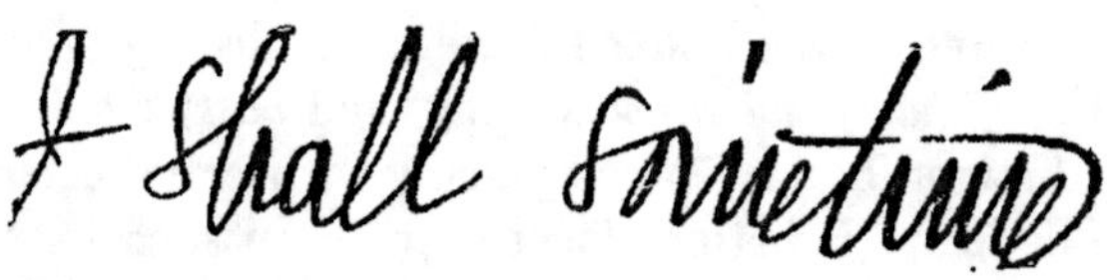

Inartistic Writing

This form of writing ranges from the laborious grind of the hard working mechanic, to the cramped

Denotes modesty, frankness, truthfulness, and sincerity. Writer is unassuming, honest, trustworthy and up-

schoolboy hand; it implies an unsophisticated nature, although writers of high intellectual attainment affect it, but it is always the hand of the unpracticed penman.

(The author of this specimen is a noted writer of children's books and kindergarten stories.)

right; a righteous, just, and morally clean nature. Lacks conceit, although possessing an unreasonable disposition.

Ornate Writing

When writing is ornamented or penned with great care and with much flourish and Spencerian shading; done for effect; conscious fancy writing.

(*a*) Although probably talented or cultured, the writer is egotistical and conceited. Inclined to be headstrong and opinionated; self-impressed with own importance and often affected in manner. (*b*) These writers are usually light-hearted and have a high perception of beauty and form. (*c*) Constructive ability, dexterity, and artistic talents are indicated. (*d*) When other signs confirm it, often a scheming, planning, enterprising, adventurous nature. (*e*) Usually small, reflective intellect.

SPEED

There are three classes under this heading, distinguished as *hasty distinct* writing, *hasty indistinct* writing, and *hasty dwindling finals.* The hasty distinct form is penned quickly with every letter perfectly legible. The hasty indistinct form is made in such haste that an occasional final letter is omitted, yet every word is readable. Hasty dwindling finals is that form wherein the last few letters in a word dwindle off into an undulating stroke, hardly decipherable, and if read at all, must be judged by *sensing* the word.

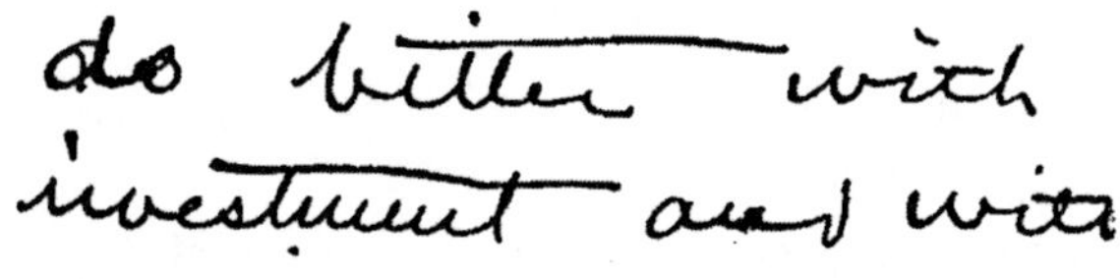

Hasty, Distinct Writing

Quickly penned with every letter legible.

(Specimen of the handwriting of a well-known public entertainer.)

Indicates quickness, animation, vivacity, with much hastiness. Intolerance of details and an inherent inability to do things according to plan and order. Usually lacks ability or aptitude for practical work. Not steadfast or ardent in the affections; generally impulsive.

Hasty, Indistinct Writing

Letters hurriedly written, some only half formed or omitted.

(Specimen of the Hon. Wm. J. Bryan's handwriting.)

The indications of this script denote much ability; one always accomplished in one direction or another. Possesses a great deal of individuality and originality. Generally good talker, and entertaining; may have oratorical ability. Usually ambitious with vividness of imagination and inspiration, and sometimes a spice of genius. When other signs confirm it, insincerity, dissimulation, and artfulness are indicated, and are present in one form or another. Conscientiousness is not strong; the tendency is toward an elastic conscience.

Hasty, Dwindling Finals

When the last few letters in a word dwindle off into undulating strokes.

The pen mark of the sharper and schemer; will not submit to dictation. Does not always intend that what is said shall be taken literally. Lacks frankness; a *finesse*, diplomatic nature; a *jollier*. Has an impenetrable personality, which will be either subtle, hypocritical, or dissimulating, according to accompanying signs.

Slow Writing

Writing that is carefully penned is not necessarily *slow* writing. The form considered here relates to writing that is carefully punctuated, with the "t" crossings deliberately made, the spacing between words equidistant, and the lines clearly separated from each other. The writing lacks snap and dash, as if every letter had been particularly placed.

This form of *slow* writing signifies a desire for care and order; the writer is neat and methodical; habits are quiescent and calm.

When the writing is slow and appears cramped or unsteady.

Advanced years or infirmity may be inferred.

When *slow* writing is straggling and spread over the lines, using more space than necessary, it is classified as *Diffused* writing, (See *Diffused writing.*)

Uneven Writing

This form of writing may be either *hasty* or *slow*; the writing varies in size with uneven base that appears broken, on and off the line, yet not *wavy*. The tops of the letters are uneven also, some higher than others, and lack uniformity. A *wavy* base line is undulating, serpentine-like; this must not be mistaken for *uneven writing*.

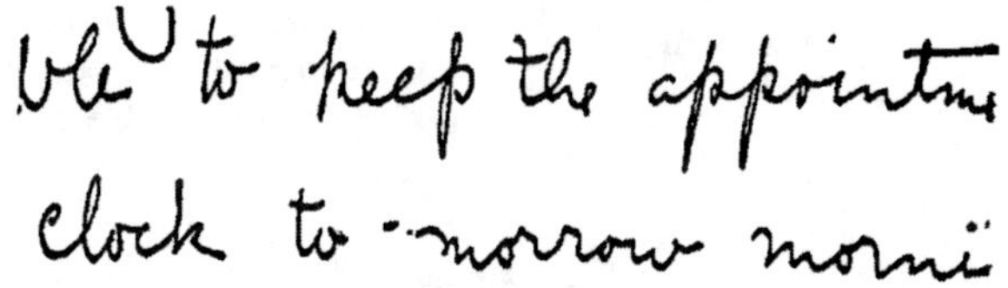

Hasty, uneven writing.

Careless in little things and not methodical or systematic. Inclined to be indifferent to engagements or business affairs.

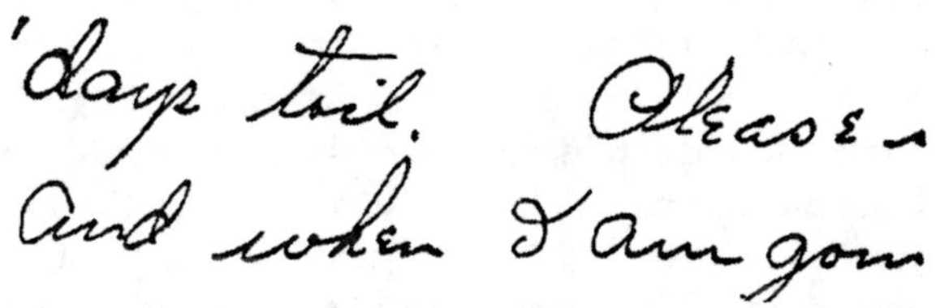

When the writing is uneven and slow.

(Specimen of a well known woman *freak*, exhibiting at the summer resorts as the "Fat woman.")

Uneven, slow writing, and particularly the *straggling* form, denotes a weak and vascillating character; lacks judgment and discretion. Little self-control; apt to be flighty and irresponsible; lacks poise and full mental balance. There is a lack also of harmony in action and of the faculties. Writers of this form are inattentive, abstracted, visionary, indecisive, unsteady, capricious, slovenly, awkward, careless, and unpractical. They are not to be depended upon.

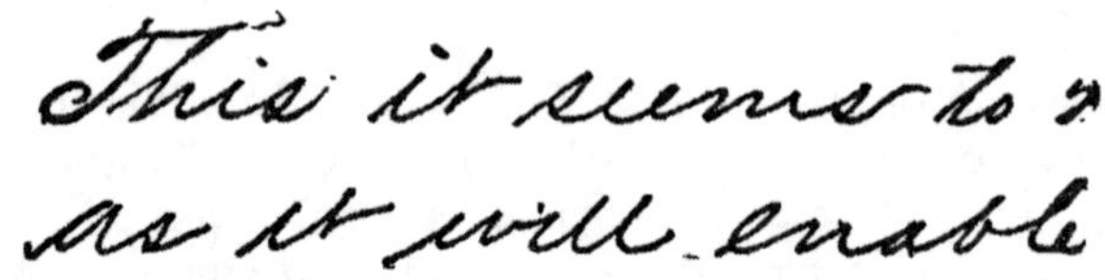

UNIFORM WRITING

Usually slowly written with all the characters uniformly penned, all one size, even base line, all down strokes at same angle, uniform spacing between words and lines.

Denotes neatness and one who acts with precision and carefulness. Always tactful, methodical, painstaking, with well-balanced faculties. Good business instincts; thrifty, prudent, and economical. Makes good manager, organizer, capable clerk.

SPACE

Space refers to the relative distances between letters and words, and also the lines. Some writers use too much space and others crowd their letters and words, and even the lines close together. One is called *Crowded* writing and the other is called *Diffused* writing. Crowded writing is that in which the letters in a word are crowded close together, jammed against each other, as if to shut out any encroachment of additional letters; or the spacing between words is so small that it makes the words appear to run together, or crowd the margins, or even use the margins for additional writing. The lines are also written so close to each other, that they could not be cut apart without mutilating the loop letters. In fact the loop letters run into the lines above and below, giving the latter a confusing, tangled appearance. The normal space at the left margin should be about one-half inch, and even all the way down the page; this gives to the letter an orderly, harmonious appearance. Good business men do not leave wide margins, and do not crowd them. The matter is written squarely on the sheet, using all legitimate space, and the loop letters are not permitted to extend to the lines above or below. This explanation defines the difference between a normally written page and one that is crowded. Diffused writing shows the letters in a word and the words themselves widely spaced and spread over the page, using more space than necessary. The form where the message is written in the center of the page, leaving wide margins at the right and the left, may not be considered *diffused*, although it takes on largely of the characteristics of diffused writing, with some modifications. Diffused writing is usually the habit of those who write large hands. Another form of diffused writing is the *straggling* variety used by the insane. This latter form is usually associated with weak, uncertain strokes, and while diffused in space is actually crowded, one line running into another, rendering it difficult to read.

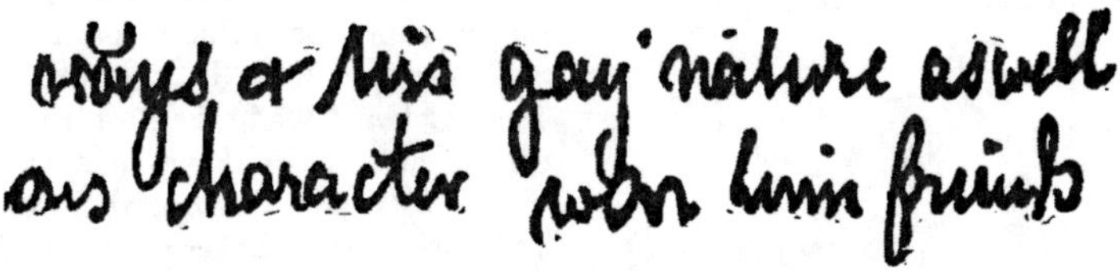

Crowded Writing

When the letters in a word and the words themselves are crowded close together, with the loops of one line running into the lines above and below.

(Specimen of handwriting of a recently dethroned European monarch.)

Inclined to worry and to be particular about little things. Tendency is to be exclusive; takes a narrow view of life. When other signs confirm it, it denotes a saving disposition, inclined to pessimism and a suspicious nature. Naturally secretive, with a cramped and warped mind. Not brilliant; moody.

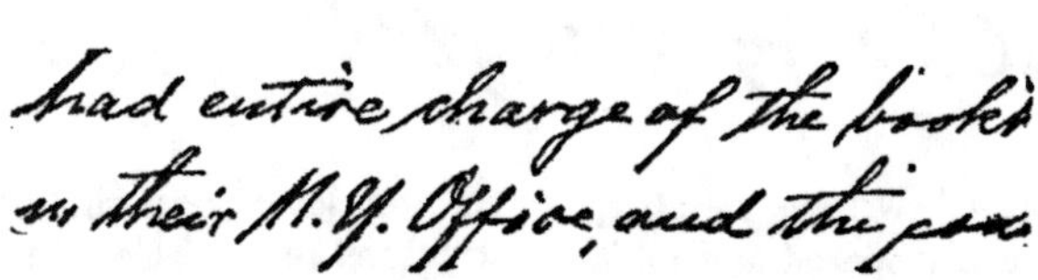

Compressed Letters

When the letters in a word are close together, not crowded, written as if they were pressed against each other.

This form of writing indicates more or less an economical disposition, and, probably, avarice.

DIFFUSED WRITING

When the letters in a word and the words are widely spaced and spread over the page.

(*a*) Denotes generosity and extravagance. Rarely economical or thrifty. Not methodical or systematic, and merely superficial in accomplishments and education (if in large hand.) (*b*) Has quick and ready mind with inherent talents. Does things in a hurry; often hasty and careless, thoughtless and imprudent; dislikes drudgery. (*c*) Lacks sound judgment; ideas are diffused and cannot easily concentrate the mind. (*d*) Is of sociable disposition, fond of company, enjoys entertaining, and being entertained. Usually good dresser—dislikes plainness.

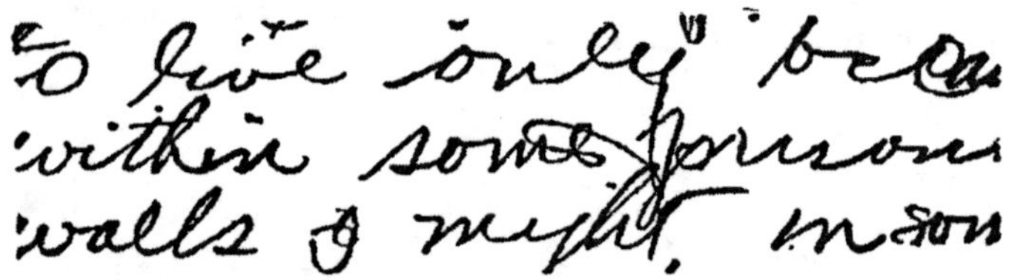

When diffused writing is straggling and badly spaced and indistinctly written.

(Specimen written by a former minister of the gospel, who was executed for murder, at Boston, Mass.)

Indicates slovenliness, with more or less mental weakness. This form of writing is characteristic of lunatics. Usually lacks strong mentality or mental vigor, due sometimes to illness or mental distress caused by grief or other mental disturbance. (Consult other features in specimen to confirm these significations.)

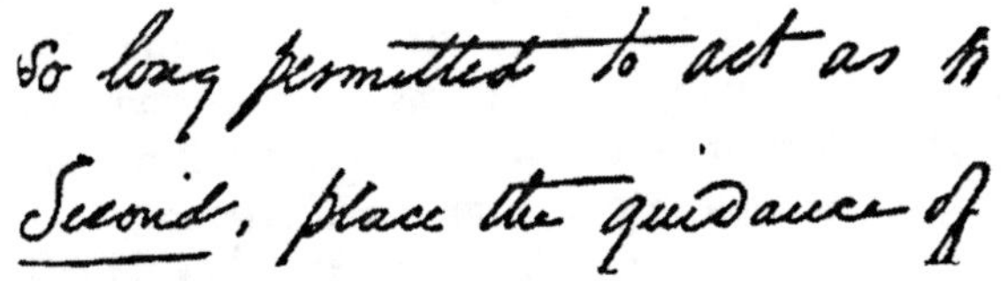

Well Spaced Writing

When the letters and the words are evenly and proportionately spaced, with lines clearly separated from those above and below.

(This is a specimen of President Woodrow Wilson's handwriting, written in 1912.)

Well-ordered mind with good judgment; one who can be depended upon in matters calling for circumspection and prudence. Rarely acts hastily on matters of business; never becomes confused or excited. His nature is conservative, with the instincts of a business man. Cannot be convinced against better judgment. Makes good manager.

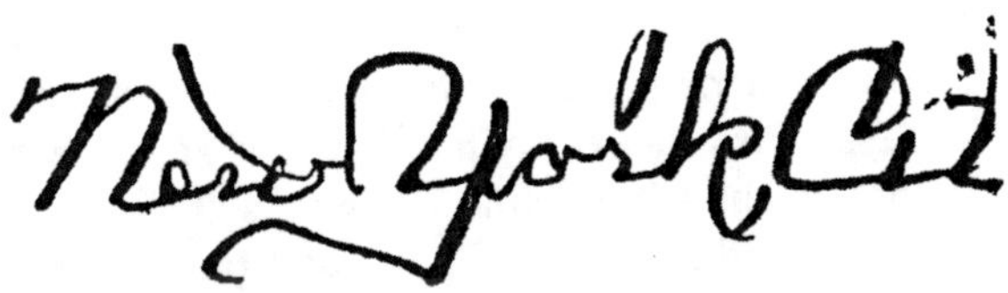

Not Well-Spaced Writing

Small letters irregularly spaced in words; spacing between words not uniform; lower loop letters running into the lines below; margins uneven; writing has a listless appearance.

Writer is careless in manner and indifferent to engagements or minor proprieties. Flighty, lacks poise; not methodical or systematic. Apt to change mind quickly and is otherwise not dependable. Decision always more or less unstable. Likely to be rash and imprudent in financial affairs. Generally speculative.

LINES

What is meant by lines is an imaginary line, more or less straight at the base, on which the letters are supposed to rest. A specimen for examination should be, preferably, on unruled paper, written in black ink. Should the specimen offered for examination be written on ruled paper it is advisable to exclude any deductions, so far as they pertain to the lines, unless it is shown that the writer has totally disregarded the ruling. This also applies to lines that appear very straight and spaced with exactness, because some persons use guide lines beneath their note paper, or even mark the lines with a ruler. Lines are divided into several classifications, each having a special significance. *A straight* line is written horizontally on the page, with even base. Tilt the paper slightly and scan down its surface, from the left to the right. If straight, the base will appear even, with no indentions. A continuity of letters and words straight on the base line accentuates the sign. *Ascending* lines cant upward, sometimes only slightly, sometimes very markedly. Some writers make ascending lines from ascending words, the words ascending more than the lines. This classification is sub-divided into lines that start to ascend and then descend; lines that descend and then ascend; lines that are formed of ascending words; lines that are formed of descending words. Another classification deals with *descending* lines. When the writing cants downward about twenty per cent off the horizontal, and it is known that the natural writing is straight, the sign is dependable. Some writers incline their words downward on descending lines, giving the base an appearance of steps; others incline their line while the words slightly ascend, or appear off the descending line. These oddities in writing are supplemented by lines that are improperly spaced and *irregular lines.* A study of the lines often provides the key to other signs and is therefore important. The lines of writing are relatively the same in importance as the keyboard of the piano, without which the graphologist and the piano student are unable to proceed. Patience and practice in either study makes the proficient performer.

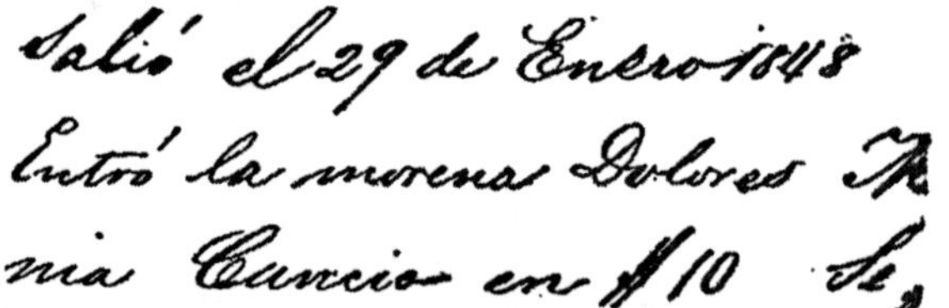

STRAIGHT LINES

When writing is placed horizontally on the page, the base being even.

General significations for straight lines are honesty and straightforwardness. When the small letters are all written equal in size, and of the same height, the signs are accentuated.

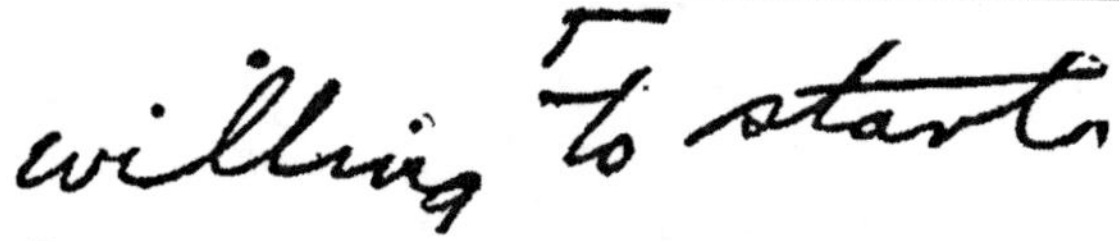

ASCENDING LINES

When the writing has an upward cant on the page.

Ambitious nature; a buoyant disposition, and lively interest in life. One who is naturally hopeful and not easily discouraged. These writers possess determination to succeed, and are constantly pushing ahead, as they allow nothing to daunt their ambitions.

When the lines ascend very markedly.

Ideals and aspirations are high; denotes an exaggerated ambition; more ambitious than practical. Likely to be visionary, with extravagant aspirations.

When lines start to ascend and then descend.

Indicates enthusiasm at first, but not enough energy to finish at end.

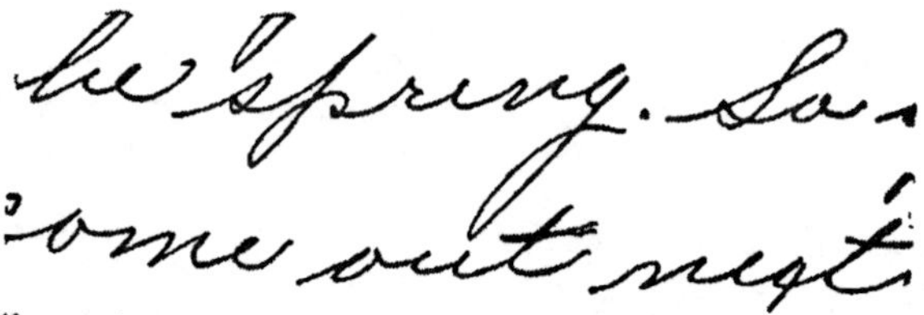

When lines descend and then ascend.

Indicates hard work to begin, takes courage, gets hopeful, and then completes the task.

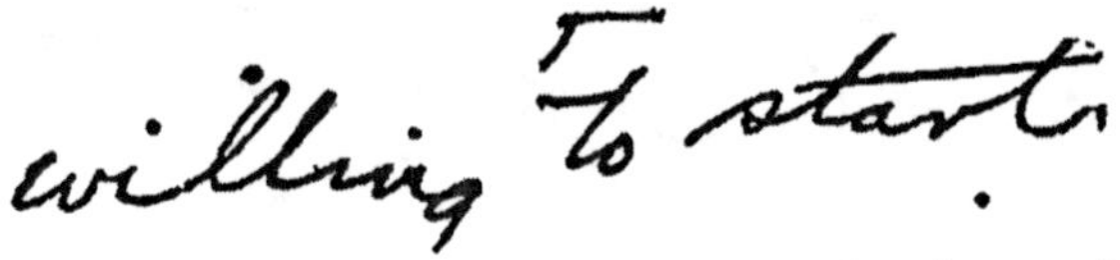

When lines are formed of ascending words.

Indicates moderation; no haste; constant consideration.

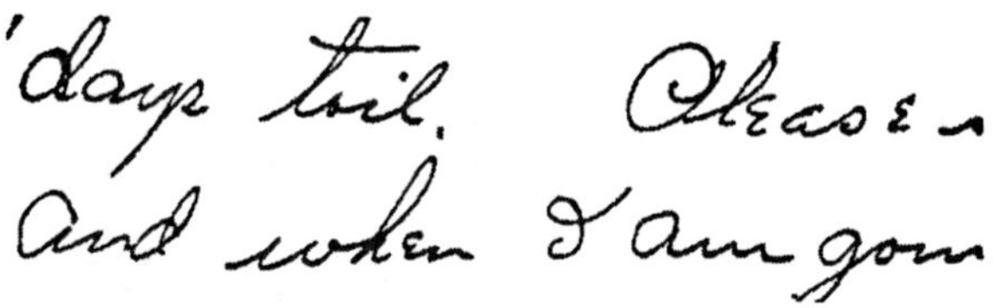

When lines are formed of descending words.

Probably an active character that will fight successfully against disappointments and discouragements.

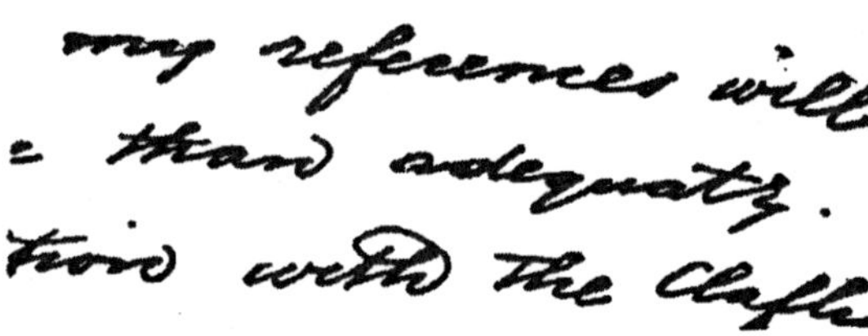

Descending Lines

When the writing cants downward off the horizontal, and it is the natural manner of writing.

There is a certain lack of initiative or active ambition; may be ambitious but lacks the necessary vigor or steadfastness of purpose to accomplish a task. Easily put out of humor; habit of fretting and worrying. Is subject to morbid prejudices. Often suspicious, distrustful, and apt to take offense readily. Happy nature and in high spirits one hour, and down in the depths of gloom and discouragement the next.

When the lines descend very markedly more than twenty per cent. downward and the writing appears weak.

The indication is of ill health, depression, or a diminution of mental vigor, due to grief, or some physical indisposition. Those who are mentally unbalanced, rarely write the descending hand.

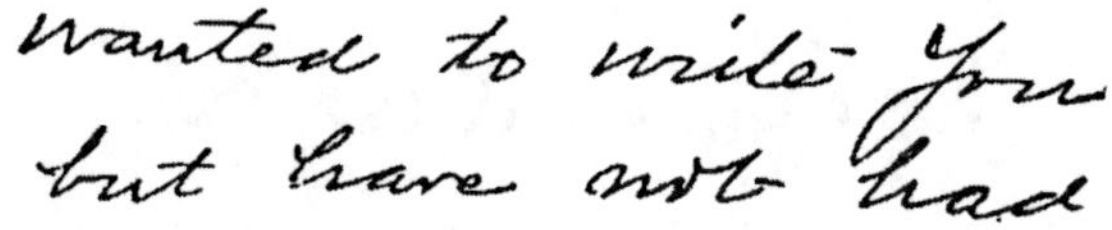

When words incline downward on descending lines. — Indicates a struggle against depression.

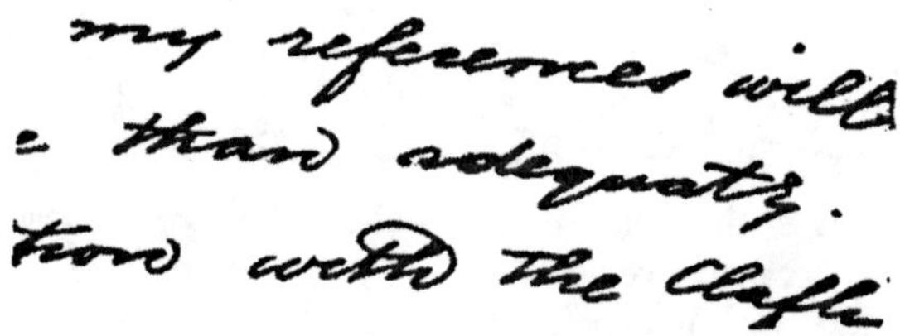

When the lines descend more than the words on descending lines. — Writer is satiated with pleasure; afflicted with ennui.

When horizontal lines end with the last words *drooping*. — Indicates one troubled with "the blues."

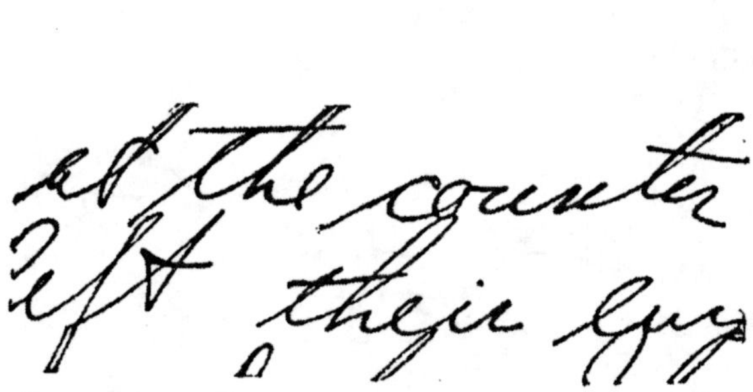

IRREGULAR LINES

When unevenly spaced in relation to one another. — Not naturally gifted with methodical or business instincts.

Irregular lines, with small letters constantly varying in size, small letters *a* and *o* closed.

Indicates deceitfulness.

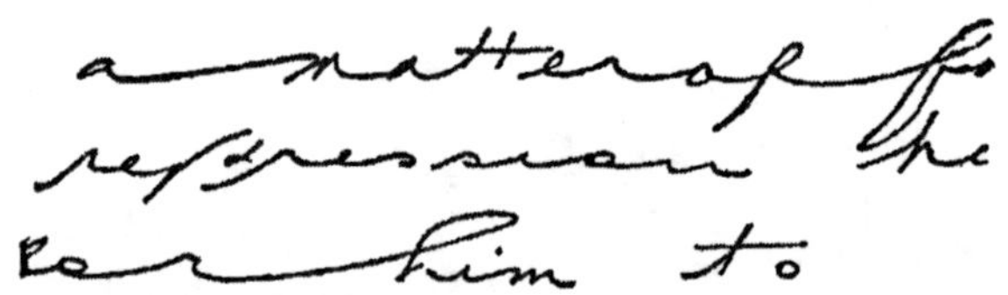

Irregular lines, with small letters, *a*, *o*, tightly closed, constantly varying in size, with tops pointed, finals never ascending to right.

Indicates cunning and trickery.

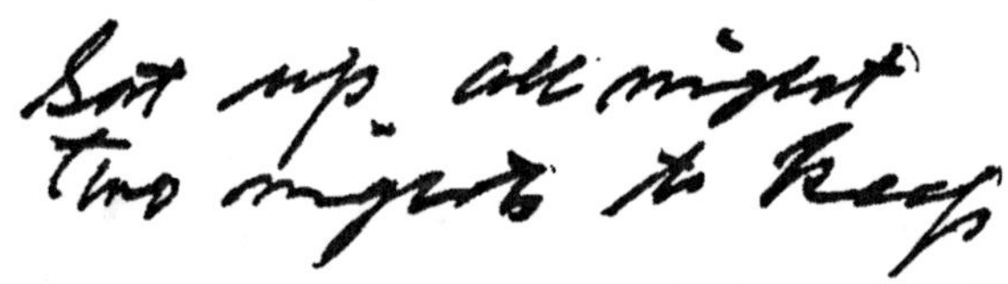

Irregular lines; letters close together; *a*, *o*, closed tight; letters constantly varying in size; hooks at end of strokes; irregularly spaced words and lines.

The indications are thievishness and a general perverted nature.

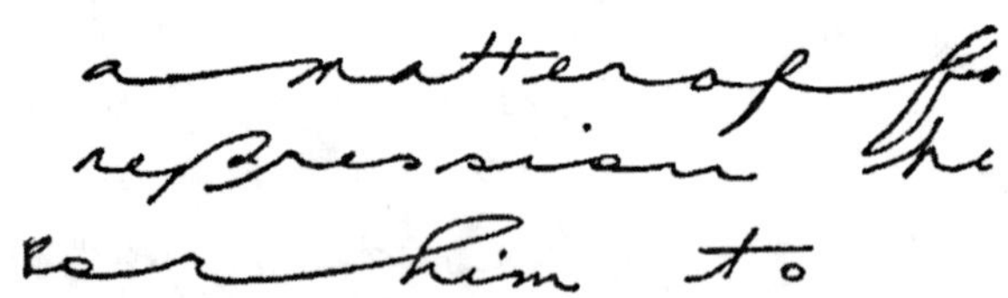

Irregular lines, an occasional straight line, some slanting upward, some downward; base lines uneven and some undulating.

Signifies deviousness.

MARGINS

In discussing this classification it is to be understood that the margins of a letter are meant. Should any other than a letter be offered for examination this classification may be ignored, unless the right margin shows drooping finals. A letter may be written by beginning close to the left side of the page and finishing close to the right edge, or a margin may be left on the left side of from one-half an inch to two inches, this variation depending on whether it is a note or letter sheet. The normal space for the left margin is about one-half an inch. Some writers place their message artistically in the center of the page, leaving wide margins on both sides of the sheet. Most women and men of extravagant tastes ignore the hyphenated word, preferring to leave open gaps at the right margin, unless they fill the space with a horizontal stroke of the pen continuous with the last word. These are idiocyncrasies that are tell-tale marks. The man who tries to save money, but spends more all the time, starts the top of his letter near the left margin, but by the time he has reached the bottom of his letter he has gradually worked away from it, until the last line is farther away from the side of the sheet than the first. Then we have the writer who reverses this manner of placing his lines, and begins wide at the top and gradually closes in toward the edge of the sheet at the bottom. This tells us that the writer can hold his emotions in check. Again there are those who are careless of little things, and who lack all appreciation of taste and refinement, who zig-zag each line down the left side of his letter, giving an uneven appearance to the margin.

The following descriptions are self-explanatory:

The Right Margin

When the margins are wide on both sides of the page.	Artistic tastes are indicated. These writers are fond of what is neat and harmonious. The desire is for originality; aesthetic taste. Apt to be self-conscious and to study appearances. Inclined to be fussy over little things and bothered with trifles.

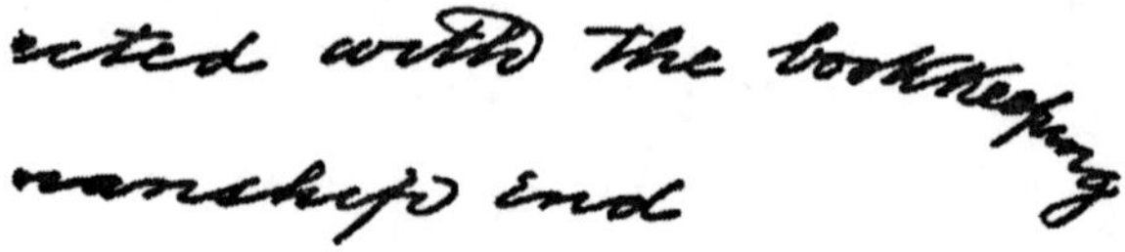

When the last word on a line "droops."

Indicates that the writer is subject to the "blues."

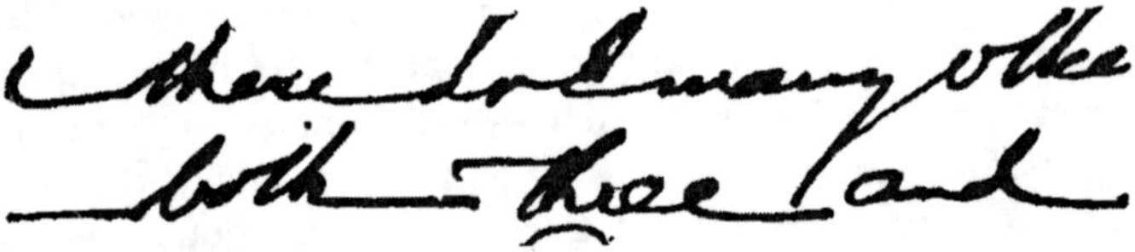

When long dashes are used to fill out the ends of lines, rather than divide a word and carry it over to the next line.

Denotes extravagant notions, with a certain degree of cautiousness and mistrust.

THE LEFT MARGIN

When the writing begins wide at the top and ends narrow at the bottom.

Inclination to spend money and to be liberal, but combats against it successfully.

When the writing begins narrow at the top and ends wide at the bottom.

Desire is to save but spends more all the time.

When the left side of the writing is uneven and lines are indented, giving an in-and-out appearance to this margin.

Lacks order; has lively nature; careless in spending money.

When written very close to the edge of the sheet, with the tops of the heading filled in, and every available spot used, even to crossing the horizontal lines, and at the margins.

Inclination is toward stinginess; usually is thrifty; lacks good taste; often untidy and sloven.

NOTE. The conventional left margin is about one-half an inch. See "Crowded Writing" for further details.

TERMINAL OR FINAL STROKES

The *terminal* of a word is the final or end of the stroke, of which there are several forms. The *abrupt* final ends as if chopped off at the completion of the last letter. The *outward* form extends horizontally away from the last letter, either in a short or a long stroke. The *upward* final may turn up in a short stem or soar above the letter. The *downward* final extends below the line, sometimes ending in a thin, short line, or is snapped down *saucilly* as if in defiance. *Downward* finals frequently end with a tiny hook as if the writer, in lifting the pen, gave it a slight jerk, leaving a little tick like appendage, that resembles a small hook. Sometimes these hooks occur in the outward or the abrupt finals, but rarely in the upward form. Some writers extend their final with the last word on a line to fill out otherwise blank spaces. A rare specimen will show finals that curve upward and back, partly inclosing the word. When these signs are habitually used in a specimen the signification is reliable. It is improbable for all the forms for finals indicated here to appear in the same specimen.

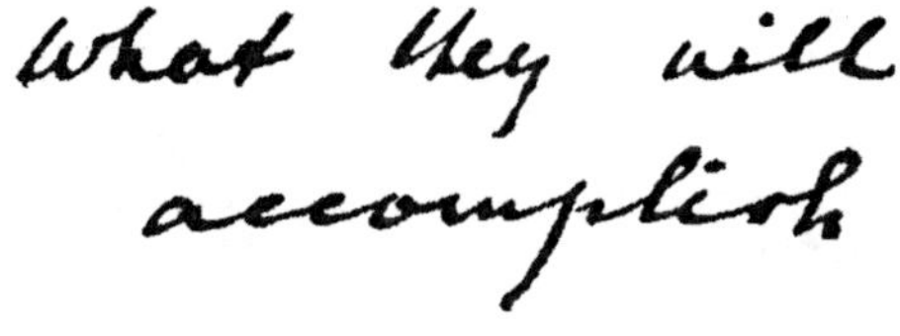

TERMINAL STROKES

Writing in which the final strokes end abruptly, as if chopped off.

(This specimen is from the handwriting of a prominent efficiency engineer.)

Generally self-contained; not given to extravagance in either the spending of material goods or of their emotions. Discriminating in generosity and kindness. Prudent, careful, reticent nature. When seen in a hand bearing evident mistrust, it denotes excessive calculation, solicitude, and extreme forethought in the character.

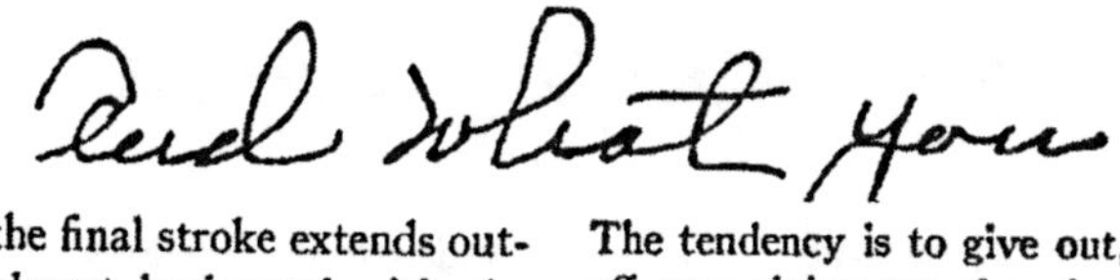

When the final stroke extends outward, almost horizontal with the

The tendency is to give out, to throw off, as a giving out of one's self for the

line, but not used to fill out otherwise blank spaces.

sake of others. Writer has vivid powers of fancy, as well as liberality and generosity. Tenacity of purpose is indicated when the finals end with a hook. When this outward final is found in a hand denoting kindliness, quick sympathies, etc., it indicates a self-sacrificing nature.

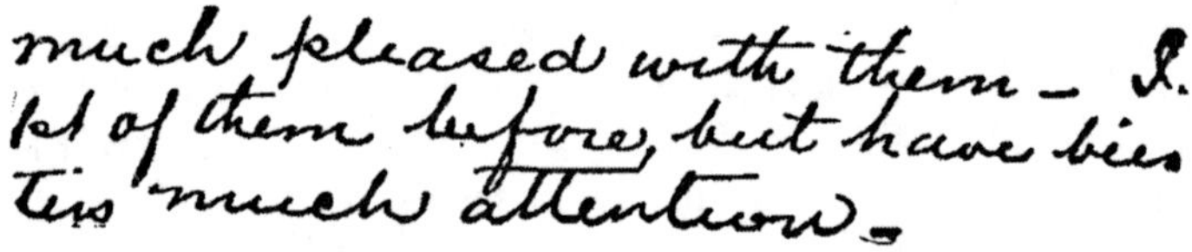

FINALS THAT EXTEND UPWARD

When the finals extend upward above the word.

Denote one who is interested in anything that tends to arouse the imagination; love of the marvelous.

When the final stroke is turned upward.

Good-natured disposition; a candid and outspoken person. Benevolence, graciousness of manner, and courteousness of bearing are also indicated.

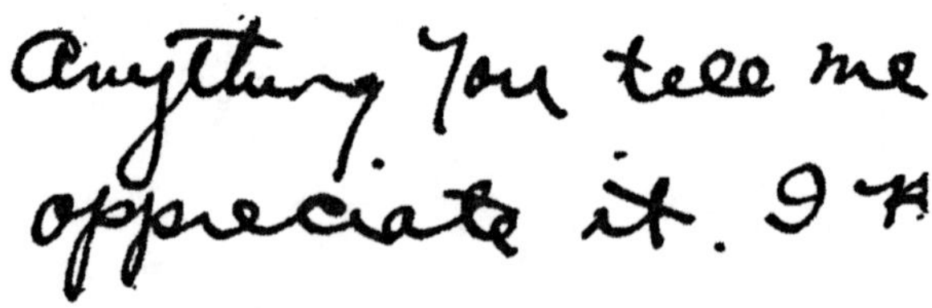

When the final stroke is turned downward without hook.

Indicates secretiveness and general lack of candor. Often obstinate and willful.

When the final stroke is turned downward with a tiny hook.

Writers are opinionated, perverse in their convictiohs, and insistent upon their own ideas. Will not tolerate dictation.

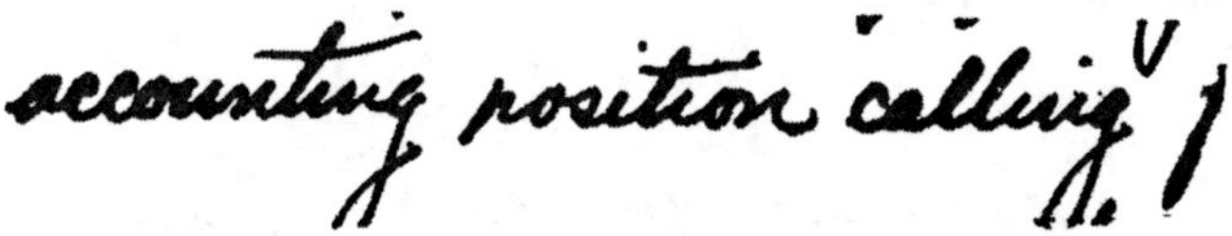

When the final stroke ends abruptly with a tiny hook.

The indication is generally determination and persistency if other signs confirm it.

When the final stroke curves up and back over the word, partly inclosing it.

The accepted explanation for this sign, is protectiveness, or the unconscious wish to shield oneself from harm, or in the interests of others.

PUNCTUATION

Few persons are able to punctuate correctly. This does not apply to inexperienced writers only, for many able writers are included in this arraignment. The features of punctuation that apply in graphology are those that indicate a total disregard of its principles, due either to ignorance, carelessness, or an aberrated state of the mind. The substitution of dashes for periods, for instance, may not be attributed to ignorance, but probably to an unconscious impulse, made while the mind was concentrated on a subject that suggested the intention to be cautious. To all intents and purposes the making of a dash might serve the writer's purpose as well as a period, but its use, nevertheless, clearly indicates a mental twist, for in graphology the intent is considered rather than the form used to express the thought. This rule applies to all features of writing, whether it occurs in the punctuation or in the letters of writing. Any departure from the established rules of writing tends to show the *state of the mind at the moment it was concentrated* on the act of transcribing thoughts to paper. Only such specimens as could not be clearly described have been introduced here, as the descriptions are generally clear and self-explanatory.

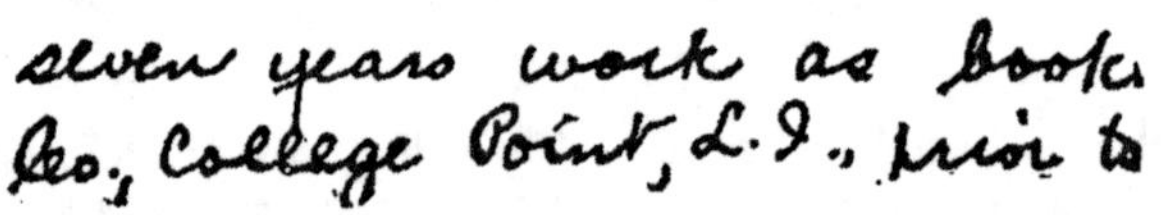

PUNCTUATION

When all marks are carefully placed, each mark properly used.

Denotes carefulness, with methodical habits. Due regard for order and a systematic nature.

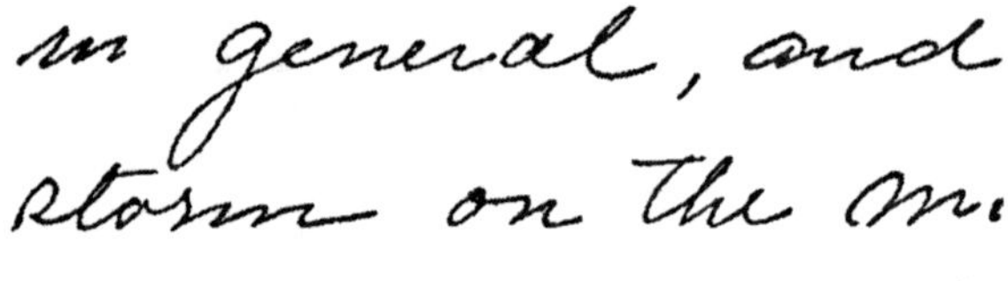

When punctuation is carelessly placed.

Indicates a general carelessness of manner and of actions.

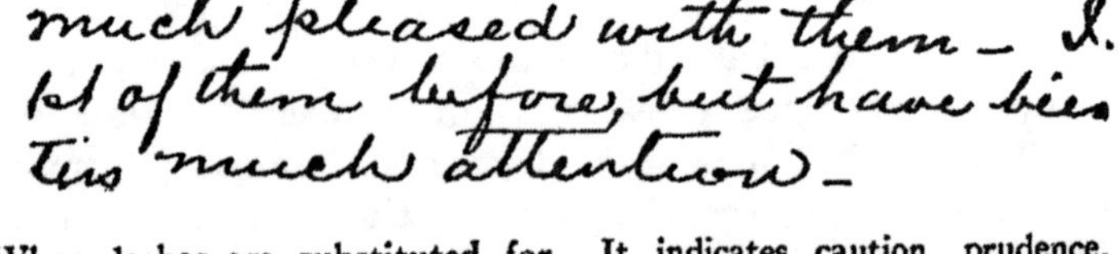

When dashes are substituted for periods.

It indicates caution, prudence, and guardedness. An aggressive temperament with a reserved exterior and manner.

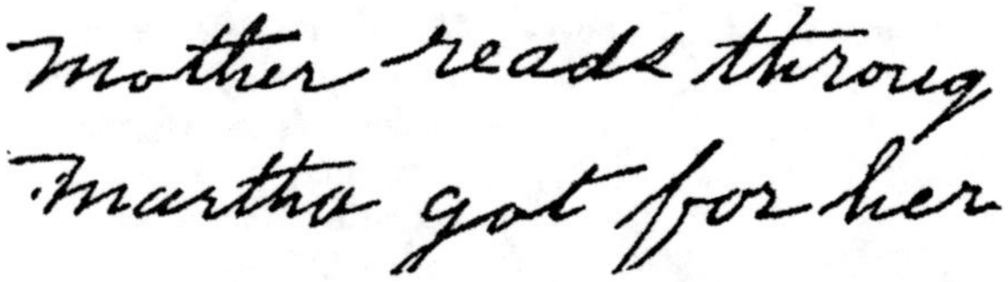

When there is an utter absence of punctuation, in the hand of the inexperienced writer.

Negligence is indicated in small matters, and lack of caution. Incompetence in the matter of detail and system. Usually denotes a bad memory.

When periods are quickly made and with elongated dashes.

Indicates excitability. This habit rarely accompanies refined hands, for culture and refinement seldom show emotion.

When periods are made with round deliberate dots.

Indicates calmness.

When exclamation, interrogation, quotation marks, and underscore are much used.

Romantically inclined. Denotes a tendency to magnify and embellish, and to become enthusiastic and wax warm over subjects that the writer has at heart.

When quotation marks are constantly and needlessly used.

Eccentricity and mental shallowness. Presumptuousness.

When punctuation marks are used accurately, especially the colon and semi-colon.

Literary ability and training usually indicated.

When the comma is persistently omitted.

Mental confusion.

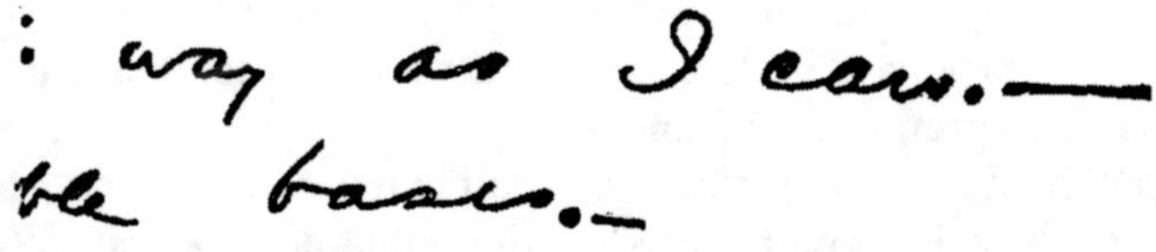

When dashes are placed at the end of sentences additional to periods.

A mistrustful and very watchful nature.

When words are constantly underscored.	Shows great desire for clearness and accuracy. Indicates self-esteem. The tendency is to exaggerate; great enthusiasm may be expected. Want of deliberation and a poor judgment are denoted.
When phrases are underscored by curved lines.	There is a delicacy of feeling and refinement of thought, some vanity and a good deal of capriciousness.
When the *X* mark is used in place of periods at the end of paragraphs.	The indications are that the writer is either a newspaper writer, has reportorial experience, or is a telegraph operator. The other signs in the specimen will indicate the classification.

CAPITALS

Capital letters may be regarded as supplementary signs to the graphological significations indicated by the small letters. The student may often find that capitals will supply characteristics that have been overlooked in the analysis of the small letters. The shape and size of capitals frequently show independent features of character, not so clearly revealed in the small letters, and in this respect are useful as confirmatory signs in making an analysis. To illustrate: Capitals that are large, high, and prominently written, with tendencies to the ornate, may indicate a certain degree of egotism, but unlike that trait found in writing with useless flourishes and with conscious shading of the down strokes in the small letters. The quality of egotism shown in high capitals may indicate a justified ego, or pride of self, due to one's station or position in the social scale, which distinguishes it from the egotism that is revealed in useless flourishes, that relate to false pride, born of a shallow intellect and an assumption of virtues unattained. Capitals are susceptible of many variations of style and of construction, each feature having definite interpretations of character, in some respects more pronounced in definiteness than that indicated by the small letters. Many authors lay great stress on the value of capitals. We once heard a French graphologist of note declare that he needed no more than the capital "*I*" as a basis for delineating character, as he considered this isolated example sufficient material for an analysis. Be that as it may, we can hardly recommend this method to the student, because every available piece of writing should be taken advantage of, if accuracy and dependability are to be assured.

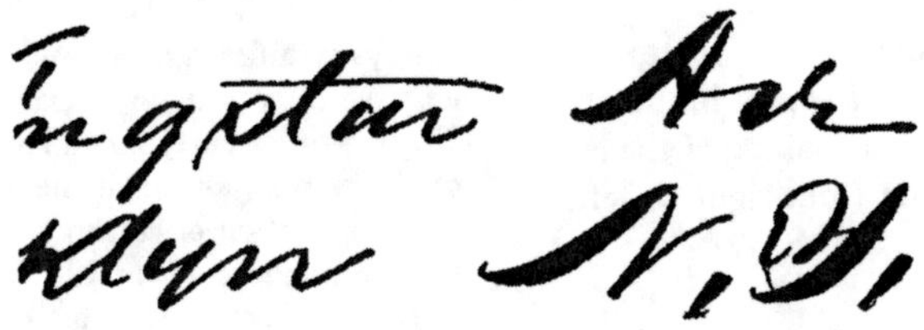

CAPITALS

When capitals are large and prominently tall, tending to the ornate, seemingly out of proportion with the small letters.

Indicates egotism, conceit, affectation, love of display, and pride. This type of writing indicates that the writer has accomplished some achievement, over which he is elated and wishes to display it. When other signs indicate it, culture and ability in some direction are shown, with vanity and egotism surely present. In one way or another the trait of self-importance, with a quietly self-appreciative nature and fondness for approbation are noted. Occasionally the traits of eccentricity and originality are evident.

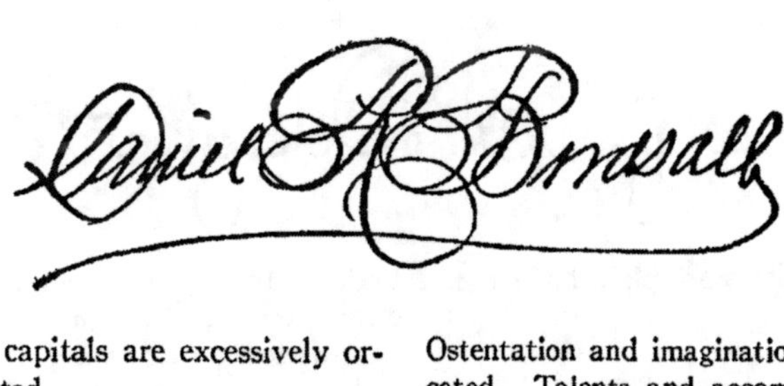

When capitals are excessively ornamented.

Ostentation and imagination are indicated. Talents and accomplishments are usually mediocre; lacking in intellectual depth.

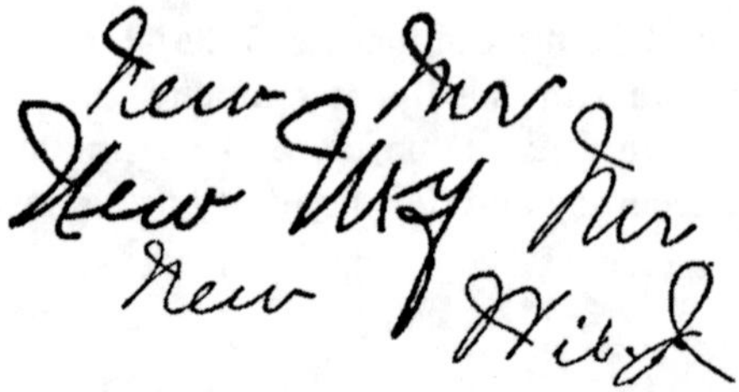

When capitals are written with the incurve, *i. e.*, an initial stroke preceding the making of the letter, and passing from right to left.

Always signifies egotism and sensitiveness with regard to social position. These writers entertain lofty opinions of themselves, although there is sometimes indication of culture and ability, if other signs confirm it. When the in-curve occurs in the small letters, it denotes unselfishness, humbleness, and generosity, but the sign always signifies sensitiveness.

When capitals are plain and simply written without flourish and almost print-like, and are not out of proportion with the small letters.

The more simple the capitals are made, the more they denote taste, refinement, modesty, and simplicity. Quiet and artistic temperaments, with inherent ability and mental culture. Literary men, deep thinkers, and philosophers usually write plain capitals.

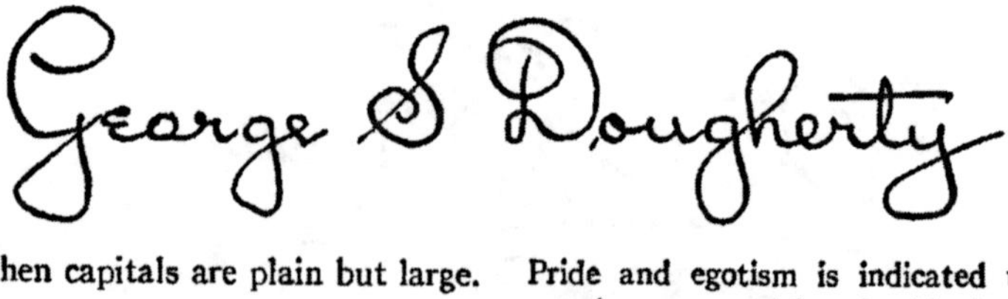

When capitals are plain but large.

Pride and egotism is indicated to a certain extent, although this is considered more an indication of boldness with some aggressiveness and masterfulness. Self-reliance is always manifested.

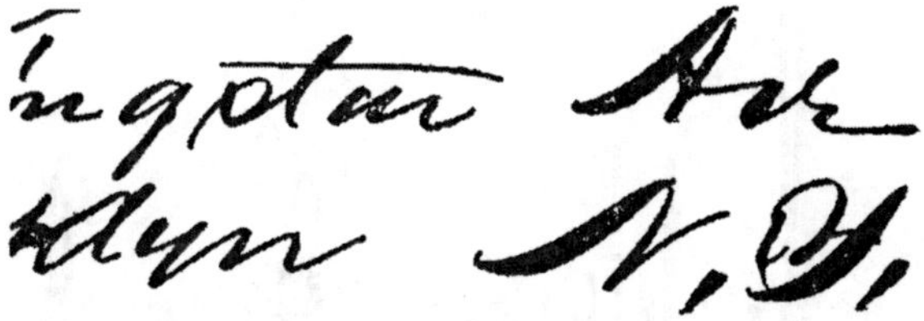

When capitals are made with heavy pressure, either in form of shading or heavy stroke.

Sensuousness and love of pleasure and comfort.

NOTE: Do not confound "sensuousness" with "sensuality." *Sensuousness* may be entirely pure, while *sensuality* is never pure.

When capitals are severely plain.

This sign is always the evidence of keen faculties.

When capitals are severely plain, of angular construction, and awkward in appearance.

Simplicity, lack of tact, and plain *homely* tastes are indicated. Practical, unemotional, and matter-of-fact persons with sterling qualities, but without magnetism are apt to use this form of capital letter.

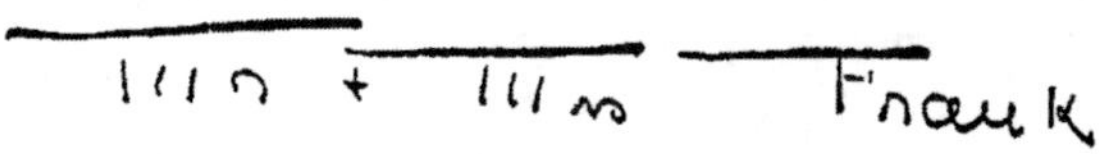

THE F IN FRANK

When capitals are made severely plain like printed letters.

Sense of form; an exacting and critical taste; some artistic ability.

When capitals are long and slender though not too high.	Pride of the unostentatious form is indicated.

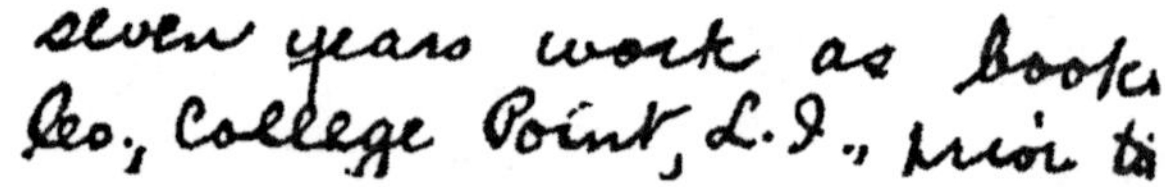

When capitals are too small in proportion to the small letters, and the writing is commonplace.	Timidity; lack of self-appreciation.

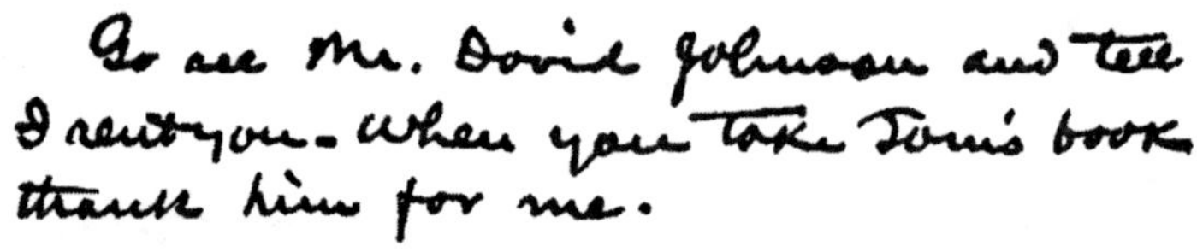

When capitals are very small with the writing forceful.	Great simplicity and fineness of nature.

When capitals are gracefully ornamented but not ostentatiously displayed.	Proud and mild ostentation, with good taste.
When capitals are disproportioned to the small letters and inharmoniously written.	Lack of mental dignity. Vulgarity of mind. Absence of literary and other refined tastes.

When small letters are replaced by capitals.

While liveliness and enthusiasm are indicated, an ignorant, bombastic pride is present. When too frequently replaced by capitals, arrogance and importance.

When capital letters are "notched," occasionally seen in the small letters.

This sign is the invariable mark for persons who are suffering with heart trouble, either valvular, or systolic murmur.

The Capitals M and N

When made in the three-stroke form like the small letter *m*.

Simplicity and freedom from ostentation is usually indicated.

When the first stroke is made higher than the others, in either form of this letter.

Pride, independence, and social ambitions (pride of family name and social position). Ambitious for the success and welfare of those near and dear.

The *M* in "Mitchell" is indicated. This is a specimen of Dr. Osler's handwriting.

When the second or third stroke is highest in this letter. Normal persons are unable to write this form of *M* spontaneously.

Denotes extravagance of mind akin to mania; visionary on religious subjects, when religiously inclined. Usually sensitive nature. Self-satisfaction. Sign of unbalanced mind; not that the writer is crazy, but invariably of a nervous, erratic, eccentric, unreasonable disposition; exacting in demands upon others; thoughtless of their comfort or capabilities. These persons usually possess a disposition that is wearing on, and trying to, others.

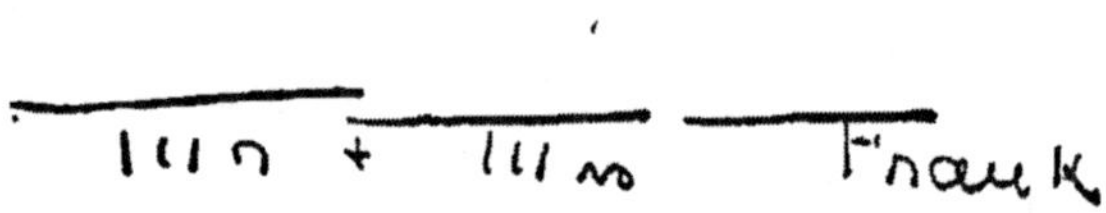

When written with three perpendicular strokes and one horizontal stroke above, sharply made.

An aesthetic nature; likes beautiful things and surroundings. Tastes are refined and artistic.

THE M IN MR.

When this letter is looped and ornamented, either the initial curves of the two-stroke form, or the final stroke of the three stroke form are elaborately ornamented or whirled into a loop.

Lack of culture; ostentation strongly marked.

When written with the incurve, the initial stroke begins at the right, swings to the left across the letter, and forms the start of the letter.

Generally persons of sensitive nature. Egotism or selfishness is indicated. A self-appreciative, proud, and self-reliant nature; if the letter is very sloping, jealousy is the characteristic.

SIGNATURES

The signature alone is regarded as undependable for an analysis, as most writers use a studied form, quite unlike the body of the text. When the signature, however, is known to have been written in the natural hand of the writer, and is similar to the body of the text, it may be interpreted freely, as no natural writing is so obscured but that the skilled graphologist may penetrate it. The descriptions of signatures given here are the average among rational signatures; anomalies and unusual forms of writing signatures have been excluded. For obvious reasons, no specimens have been reproduced here, the descriptions supplying all practical needs.

When the signature is plainly written, and similar in form to the body of the text.

The nature is ordinary, quite of the conventional type; simplicity, clearness of mind, with a personality that is modest and unassuming.

When the signature is dissimilar to the body of the text.

There is a general feeling of superiority and importance.

When the signature is smaller than the body of the letter.

Indicates a personality that is mild and without force.

When the signature is larger than the body of the letter.

Much pride and forcefulness.

When the signature is in the backhand and the body of the letter is in the right slope.

Writer is really affectionate but does not wish to appear so. Sometimes this sign denotes *importance.*

When the signature is in the forward slope and the body of the text is backhanded.	Apt to be effusive and demonstrative, but is not really affectionate. Coldheartedness is the rule.
When the signature is written with a complicated flourish.	Mistrust and subtlety of nature. When formed of intertwined lines, an intriguing personality may be expected.
When the signature is made with an elaborate flourish.	Vanity, love of display, ostentation, affectation, and boastfulness are indicated.
When the signature is made with an underlined stroke.	Self-confidence and importance justifies the sentiment.
When the signature is underscored with flourishes.	The writer is expecting to be applauded and desires approbation.
When the signature is underscored by a thick straight line.	Courage is indicated. Some degree of sensuality, which may be determined on examining the pressure used on the pen, throughout the writing.
When the signature is underscored with one straight line.	Moral courage and refinement are shown. Prudence and that sense of reputation and character that is upheld at all costs.
When the signature is underscored by two heavy straight or slightly curved lines.	The desire is for dominating others.
When the signature is underscored with a single line ending at right or left of the line, with a small hook.	Indicates tenacity of purpose.
When the signature is underscored by a curved line, beginning and ending in a sort of looped hook.	Love of admiration, coquetry, and often a love for flirtation; generally self-complaisant.

When the signature is underscored with perpendicular zig-zag lines.	Great brilliancy and originality; activity of a very pronounced description.
When the signature is inclosed by a sweeping stroke.	Impenetrability; self-interest; excessive secretiveness—sometimes a penurious nature.
When the signature is lacking any form of flourish.	Want of self-consciousness, proper pride, dignity, and freedom from all show.
When a flourish is placed at the top of the signature.	Mild eccentricity, exaggeration, and mental vanity.
When the signature is made with a wavy curved flourish for the underscore.	Denotes a witty, mirthful turn of mind, in high spirits and good humor.
When a period or a dash appears after the signature.	Evidence of caution and prudence, carefulness and mistrust.

THE SPECIAL FEATURES

Specifically the Small Letters of Writing

In the preceding chapter the general features of handwriting were discussed and the fundamentals of writing explained. This chapter is devoted to the special features, which include the small letters of writing and their sub-divisions. It is estimated that ninety per cent. of writing is done with the small letters, and in consequence one becomes familiar and adept in writing these small characters. The amount of physical and mental effort required to form these small letters are almost nil, as compared with the infinitesimal fraction of a moment more required to make the capital letters. This difierence in time between the writing of a small letter and the writing of a capital is due to the greater practice one gets in writing the small letters. This is the graphological reason why more significance attaches to the small letters than to the capitals. Strange as it may seem, the average person will unconsciously balk at making a capital letter, even if for only a fraction of a second, while no hesitancy precedes the making of a small letter—it is "habit personified," as much the part of the individual as is his sight or speech. It is proverbial with the inexperienced writer to make the capital letters inharmonious, ill-shaped, and sometimes grotesque, while the small characters are formed in a natural manner. The following divisions of handwriting deal with the "super-signs," so full of meaning to the analyst. It brings us closer to nature, closer to the creative faculties in man, which civilization and training have bequeathed to him.

ABDUCENT WRITING

There are two supplementary forms of handwriting that have special reference to the small let- The general signification of this form of writing is amiability, and a keen mind.

ters, and which govern every feature described in this division. One form is called the *abducent* style, in which all the down strokes bend inward to the left, causing all the tops of the letters to be pointed or sharp. It is made by versatile penmen with an easy swing of the pen.

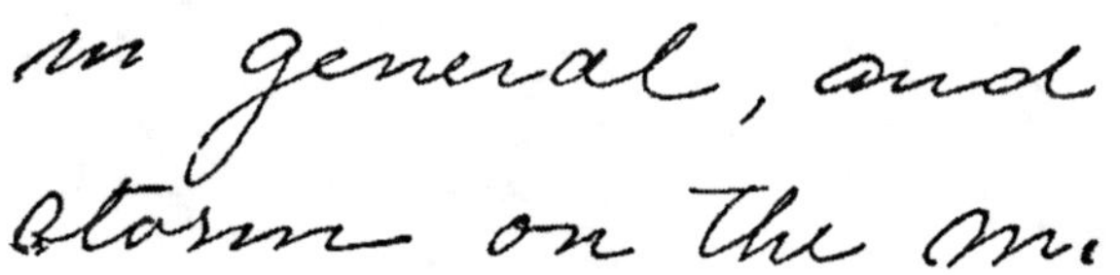

ADDUCENT WRITING

In this form all the down strokes are out-curved or bend to the right, causing the tops of the letters to be rounded, with a sharp or pointed base. Angular writing is not included in this classification.

The general signification of this form of writing is calmness, with a certain dullness of perception.

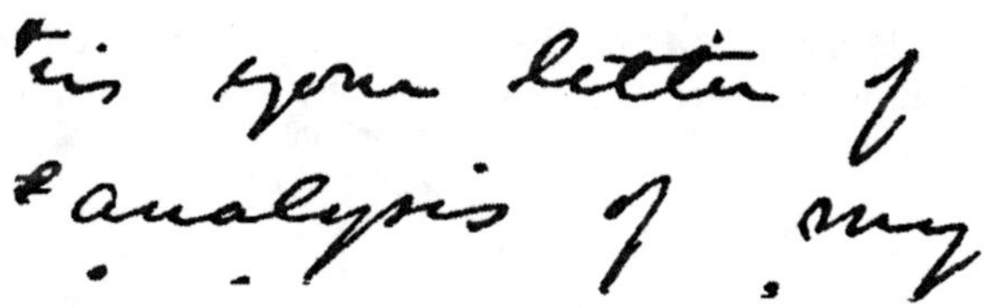

CONNECTED LETTERS

When all the letters in every word are written with one continuous stroke of the pen, each letter joined to the succeeding letter, without lifting the pen from the paper; this includes the joining of

Connected letters in writing imply logical reasoning powers. The writer has a practical turn of mind, instinctively careful, and prudent. Does not make up his mind hastily in matters of importance. Natural reasoner, for

the capital to the succeeding small letter.

he takes little for granted and is inclined to ask questions and to insist on knowing the *why* and *wherefore* of every proposition. Usually argumentative and skeptical of what is not at once understood. These writers accept very little on faith, but must be shown, for they are all "Missourians." They are generally opinionated and have decided views.

When words as well as letters are connected.

Hard to convince; tenacious of opinions; insists on a full understanding of things. Governed by judgment and reason; rarely jumps at conclusions. Views are always fortified by reason, facts, and argument. Keen, shrewd, and exacting in business matters; difficult to overreach such a person.

When words are joined together with a continuous sweep of connecting finals.

The infallible sign of stubbornness, obstinacy, and a willful, tenacious hold on opinions. Apt to be fussy and particular of details.

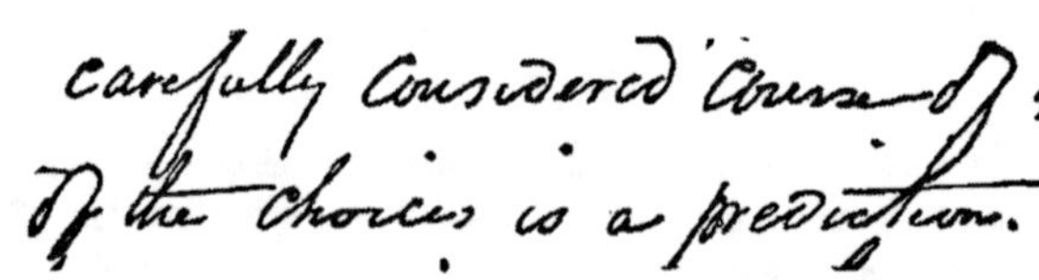

DISCONNECTED LETTERS

When there is frequent or occasional separation of the small

Signifies intuition. The writer is apt to jump at conclusions, and to make up his

letters in a word, disconnecting the characters by lifting the pen in a word before its completion. Usually in hasty or in the cultured hand; largely a woman's trait.

mind quickly and on the spur of the moment. Arrives at decisions instinctively. Judgment of matters and people is dictated by an inner consciousness rather than by any process of reasoning; quick of comprehension, observant, critical; little escapes their notice. As a rule a good judge of character. Likes and dislikes are formed on the spur of the moment, for he is guided largely by impressions; the first impressions are most reliable. These writers are nimble witted, have excellent insight, and are not easily deceived, for they grasp problems readily and will resent argument or criticism or any analysis of their opinions by others. They are satisfied with their own view of things, and will not be contradicted. Naturally religious, for their leanings nearly always tend to the spiritual, occult, or the mysterious.

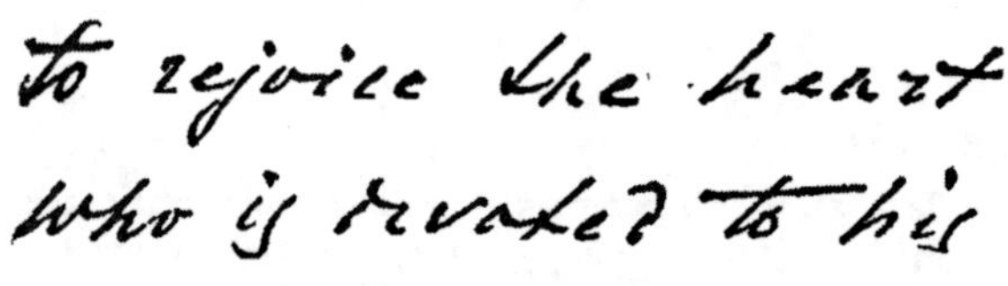

When the disconnections are very marked.

(This is a specimen of the handwriting of Paderewski, the eminent pianist.)

These writers are rarely practical or logical in their deductions. Acts and words are largely inspirational. They are idealists, guided almost wholly by imaginations, impressions, and a subconsciousness of mind that is psychical in nature. In fact, the writers are gifted with psychic powers, whether conscious of it or not. Artists, poets, musicians, orators, or those whose work is essentially inspirational, write with very marked disconnected letters.

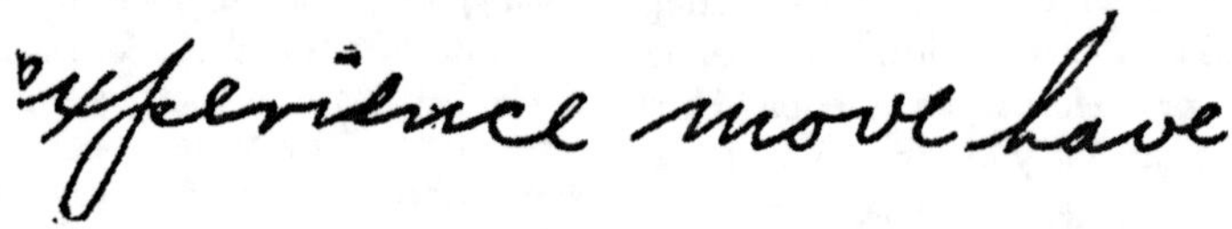

INCREASING SIZE OF LETTERS

When the last letter in a word is larger in size than the first letter.

Reliable sign for conscientiousness. These writers are naturally honest and straightforward. They place high standards for what is right and just, and will not swerve from them. They value consistency and allegiance to principle beyond price. Decision on any question is determined by principles involved, whatever the circumstances. This sign is rare.

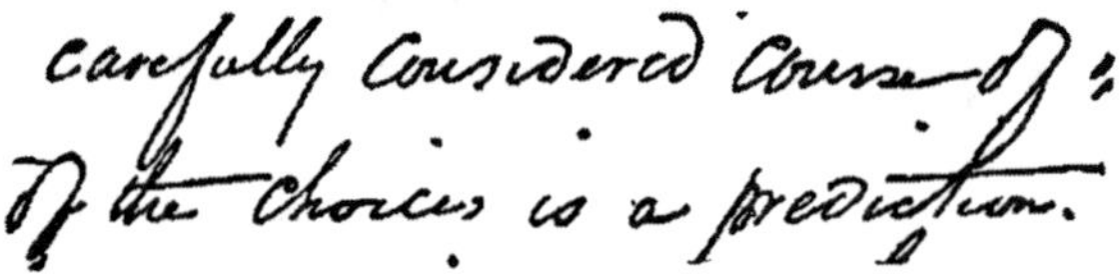

DECREASING LETTERS

When the last letter in a word is smaller than the first letter, giving the word a wedge shape, as if running to a vanishing point.

Denotes a diplomatic, tactful, shrewd, very reserved character. There is nearly always evidence of lack of candor and of frankness, for these writers regard expediency of more importance than consistency or adherence to principle. They may have conscientious scruples, but these are never obtrusive or allowed to interfere with their plans or wishes. This hand is frequently observed in business men of large capacities in the financial and extensive manufacturing interests. The captains of industry are rarely exempt from this sign.

When the last few letters in a word dwindle off into mere horizontal strokes, causing the word to be almost indecipherable.

Finesse and an impenetrable personality are indicated.

VARIABLE SIZE OF LETTERS

When the small letters are written in varying sizes, although the base line is even. This form of writing is unlike the manner of making the letters, shown under *Uneven* writing.

Persons who write their letters in this manner are versatile, with the natural ability to do many things well. Generally they lack poise, are rather changeable, and are subject to whims and fancies. There is mobility of feelings with mental plasticity and sensitiveness, and a certain amount of inconsistency, indecision, hesitancy, weakness, and sometimes untruth, should confirming signs indicate it.

TOUCHED-UP LETTERS

Writing in which some of the letters have been incorrectly or indistinctly made and which the writer has attempted to correct by going over with the pen.

Love of perfection; desire for improvement. A careful person.

(The first *l* in *Personally*.)

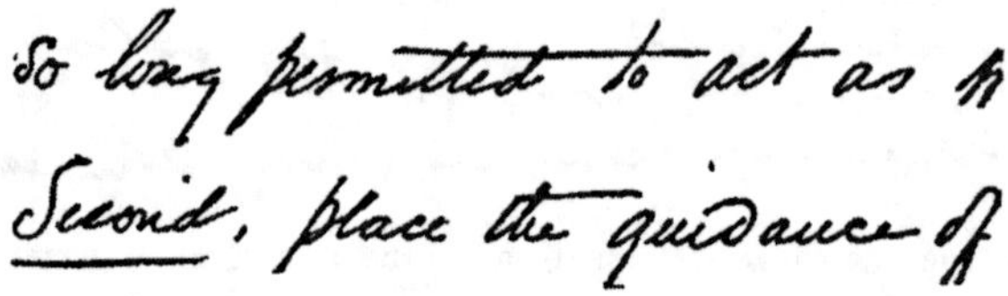

Initial Strokes

The beginning strokes of a letter. When words begin without initial strokes.

Indicates one having patience and capable of self-control.

When a letter begins with a little *tick* or tiny upstroke.

Signifies quickness of temper.

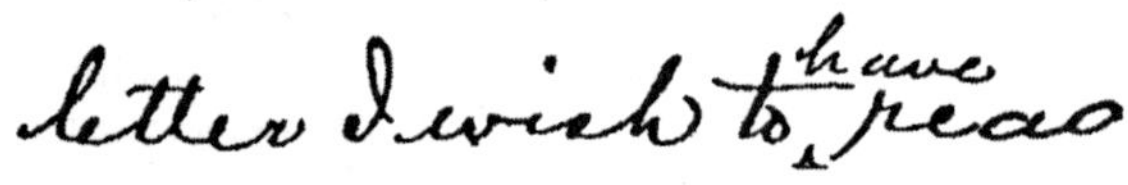

When the letters begin with a tiny *hook*.

Desire for acquisition, love of possession, usually an egotistical nature.

See the *l* in *letter*, the *w* in *wish*, and the *h* in *have*.

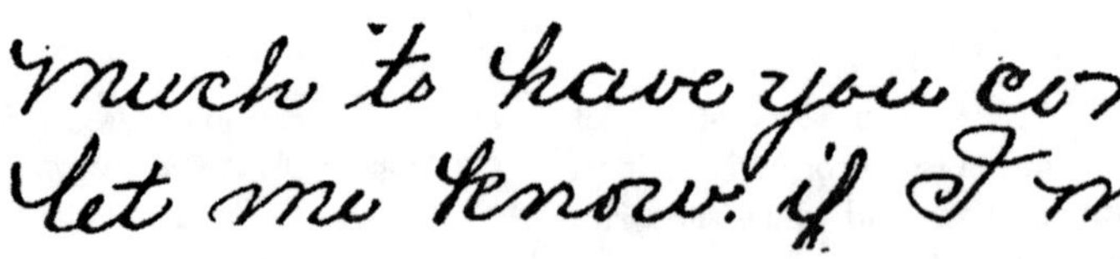

When letters begin with a curved or fancy stroke.

Powerful sense of humor; love of the ludicrous. Buoyant and mirthful spirits. A wag.

When letters begin with a long, inflexible stroke.	Impatience. Love of contest; a quarrelsome, contentious nature.

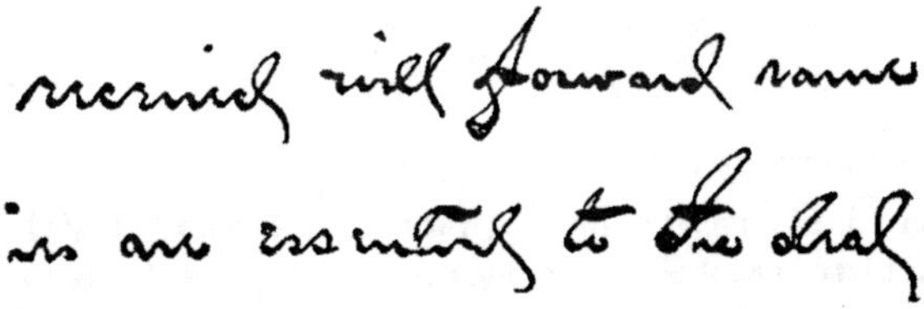

MUDDY WRITING

When the down strokes are coarse, thick, smeary, untidy, occasionally splotched. Usually occurs in shaded writing, but may appear in any style of writing.	The nature tends to œstrual, immoral habits; a sensual temperament. Usually brutal, mean, selfish, with animalistic tastes. An amative and alimentive nature. A lively imagination and quick witted.

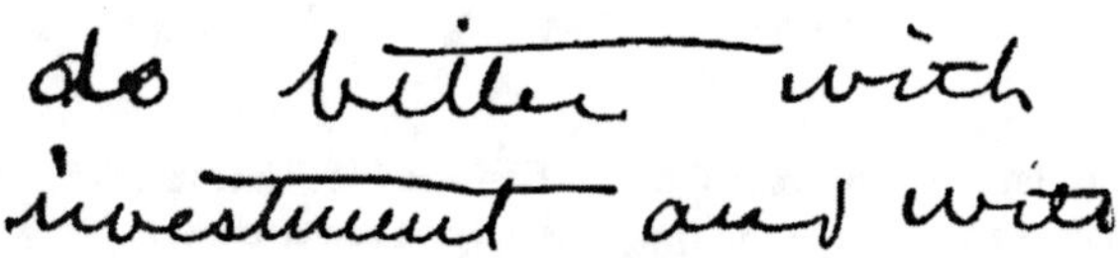

SMALL LETTERS POINTED AT THE TOP	Signifies keen intellect with an acute perception.

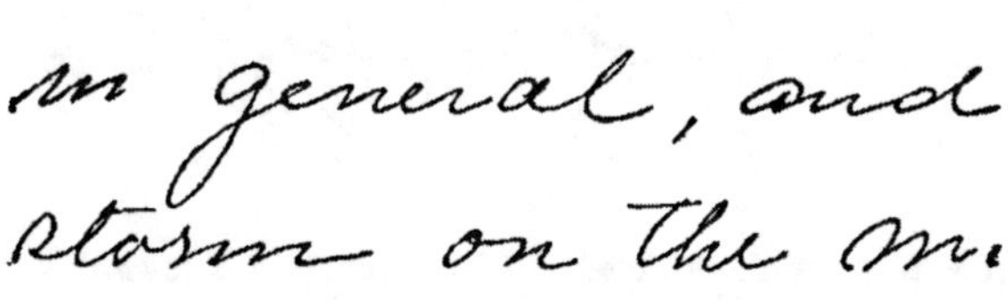

SMALL LETTERS ROUNDED AT THE TOP	Signifies a certain dullness of perception.

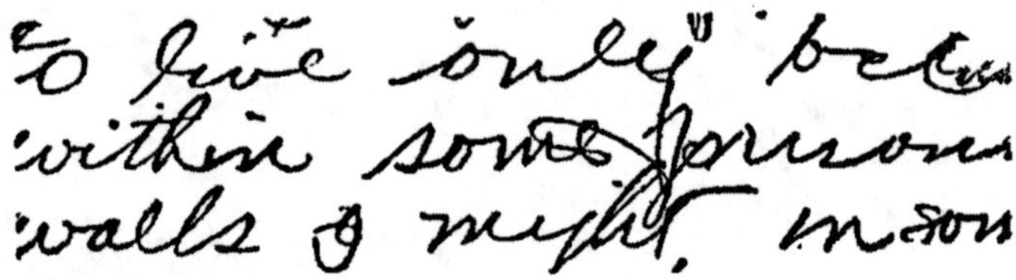

Divergent Letters

When the long letters are written at different angles.

The indications for this form of writing are a conflict between the dictates of the head and the heart.

The Looped Letters

Those that rise above the line and those that extend below the line; the letters that have graphological value are: *b, d, f, g, j, p, t,* and the *y*. Loops may be written high or low above the line, or short or long below the line. Sometimes these letters are made in the form of a stroke, either weakly or heavily written. Tiny hooks may occur at the end of *strokes.*

When loop letters are more developed above, than below the line.

Denotes idealism; mental and spiritual interests are strongest.

When loop letters are more developed below, than above the line.

The inclination is toward business and technical pursuits, with sportive proclivities.

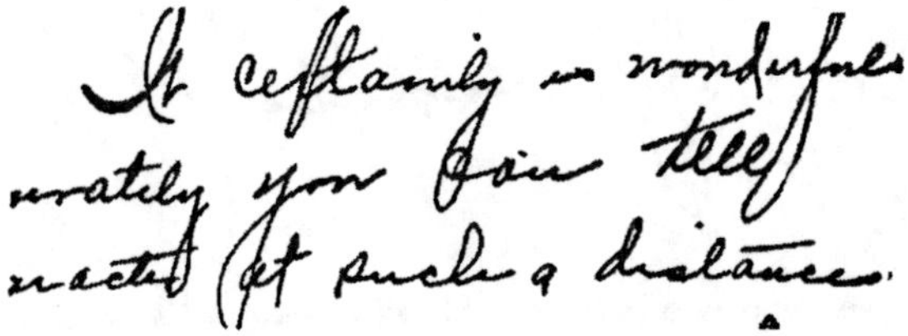

When loop letters are well developed above and below line.

Indicates a strong imagination; enterprise, organization ability, and self-consciousness are shown.

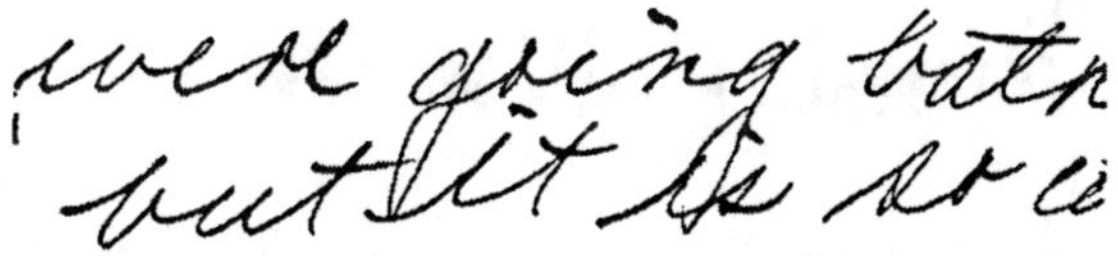

When the loops are long and extend to the line below.

Inclined to be romantic and notional, and to hold unconventional ideas on many subjects. Fond of novelty and originality—whatever is odd, appeals. Not much business ability is indicated, because these writers are too venturesome and speculative, and apt to be restless with a desire for frequent change and variety.

When the upstrokes of the lower loop letters curve well to the left.

This sign indicates clannishness.

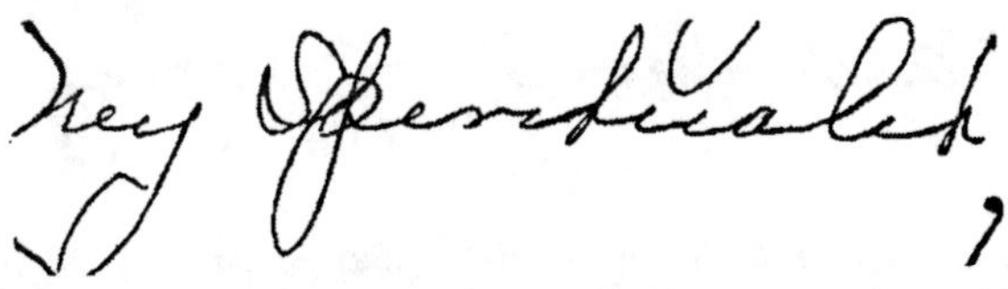

When the lower loops are long and rounded.

Fond of poetry, music, art, or whatever appeals to the imagination, along cultured lines.

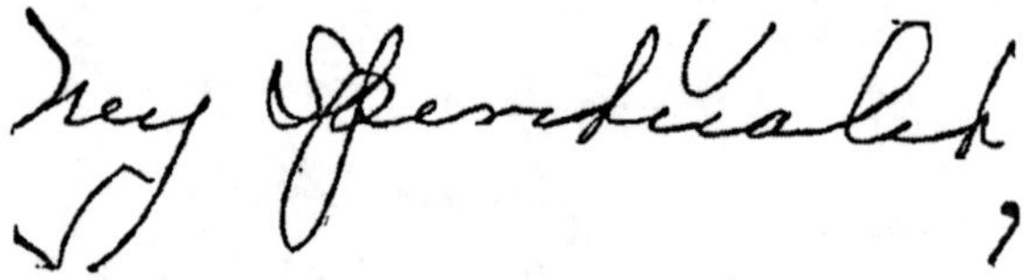

When the lower loops are *inflated*, that is, wide and balloon shape	Shows cleverness, lively imagination; a quick and vivid fancy.

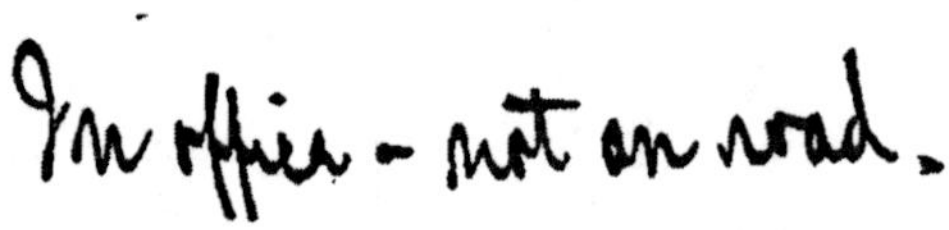

When the lower loop letters are made with a stroke without a loop.	Conservation of ideas; practical and methodical traits; a good deal of firmness, will power, and self-reliance. Some imagination is present, but it is held in check.

When the lower loop letters are made in the form of heavy strokes.	Much firmness and determination. Inclined to be obstinate; hard to convince.

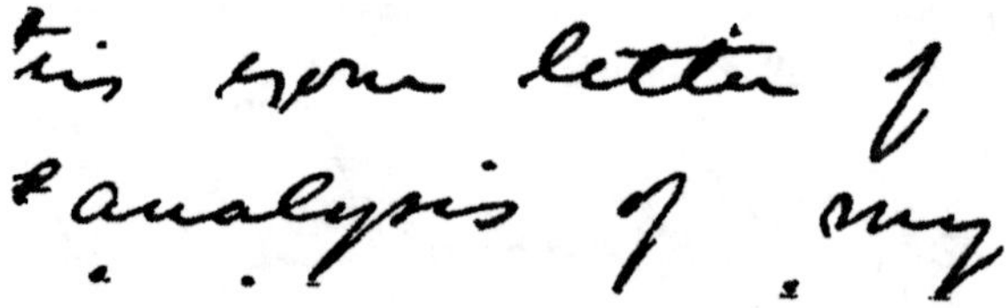

When the small letter *f* is made with the return stroke to the right —not looped.	(*a*) Indicates hastiness; desire to finish a task quickly. (*b*) A sympathetic and kindly nature; an amiable disposition.

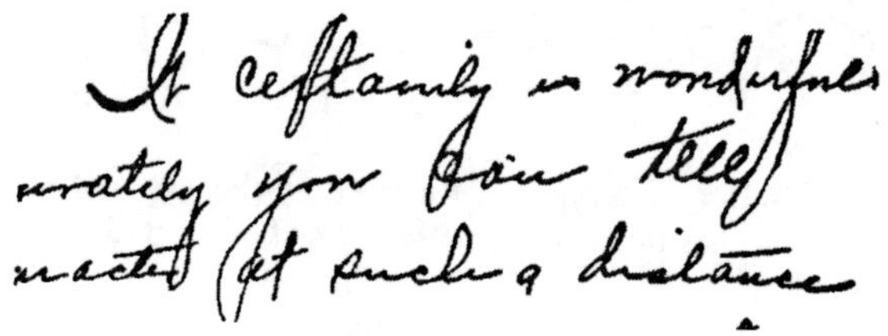

When the small letter *f* is made with very round, inflated loops.

Love of pleasure; lack of reflectiveness. When other signs confirm it, this *f* denotes energy and love of success. This style of *f* will often be found in the script of salesmen, commercial travelers, theatrical publicity men, and advertising writers, or of those whose natures are buoyant and care-free.

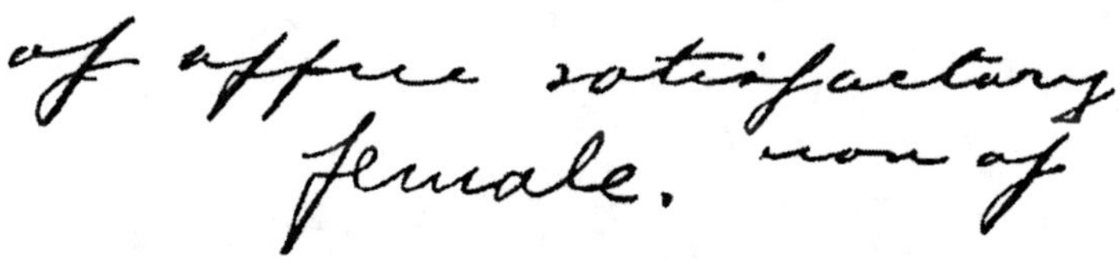

When the small letter *f* is made with the return stroke turned sharply to the left.

A lazy, indolent nature. May have sympathy and be kindly disposed, but it is not obtrusive. The disposition is vindictive and revengeful.

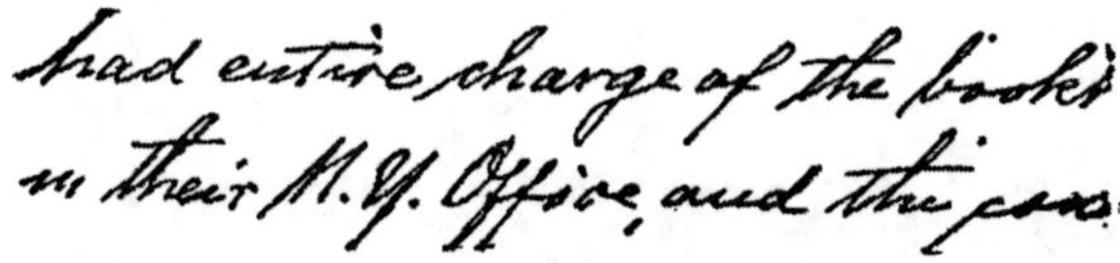

When the small letter *f* is made with the upper part looped and the lower, in a stroke.

When the stroke is light and weak, it signifies a frail and timid nature; if strongly made, a vivid imagination.

When the small letter *g* is made like the figure *8*. This form of *g* is always quickly made.

Rapidity of thought and probably of speech may be expected.

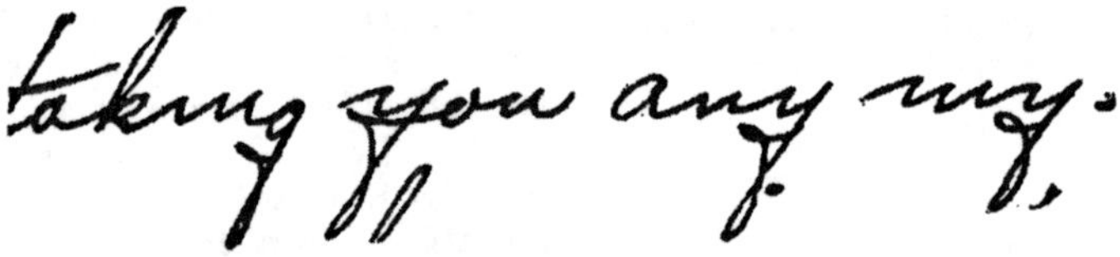

When the small letter *g* is made with a triangle within the lower loop (found in the *y* also.)

Vanity and ceremoniousness. One who is very particular about trifles. Obstinacy is shown, often accompanied by fanatical notions.

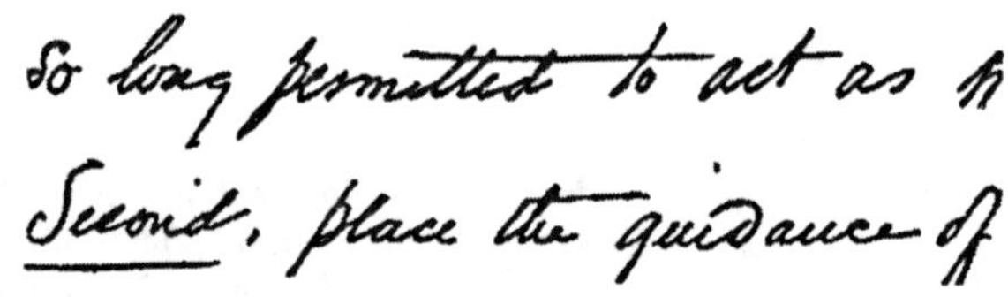

When the small letter *g* is made with the lower part a strong stroke, instead of looped.

Determination and will power.

When the small letter *g* is made with the return stroke curved up on the right (found in the *y* also.)

Generosity of affection is indicated, with an amiable, sympathetic, and kindly nature.

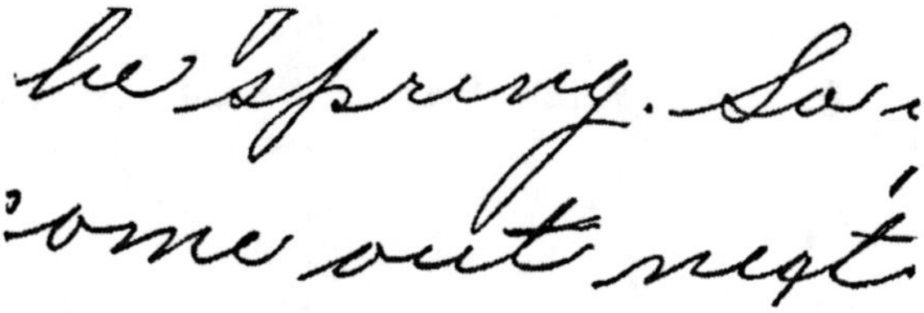

When the *g* loop is excessively long.	The tendency is to exaggerate.
When the small letter *y* is made with the return stroke to the right (shown in the *g*.)	Generosity of affection with amiable, sympathetic, and kindly nature.

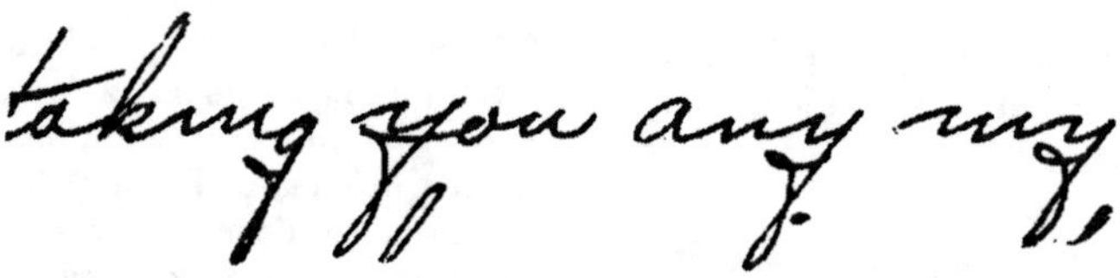

When the small letter *y* is made with a triangle within the loop.	The same as for the *g*.

When the small letters *g* and *y* are made with a flourish within the loop.	Strong likelihood of some bad moral habit existing, such as a drug addict or some kindred weakness.
Small letter *y* when it ends in a stroke, is the same as that credited to the *g*.	

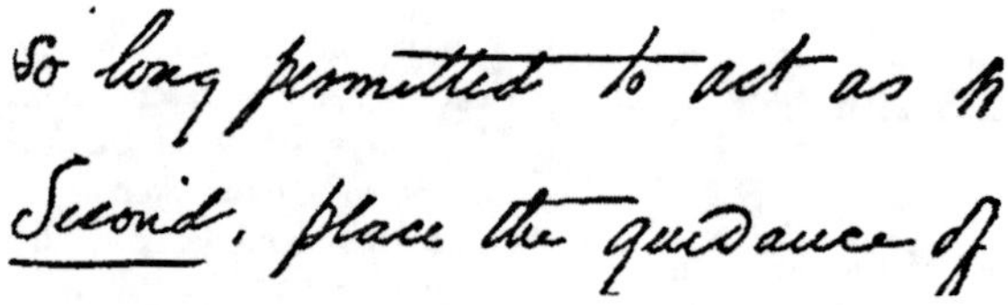

When the small letters *g* and *y* are finished with a stroke, and end with a tiny hook.	It indicates great tenacity of purpose.

Individual Letters

These have reference to the small letters *a, b, d, e, i, m, n, o, p, s, t.*

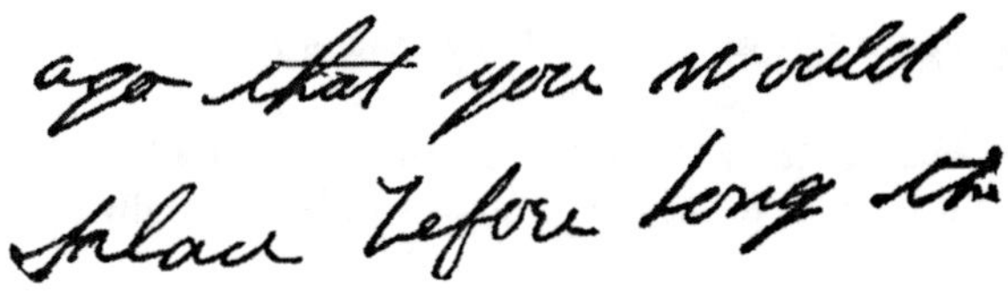

The small letters *a, o, d, g,* when written with the tops left open, not closed.

(The writing in this classification must be spontaneous to have any consideration.)

Writers who leave the tops of these letters open, are of a frank and outspoken nature, who do not hesitate to express opinions and feelings freely. It is difficult for them to keep a secret, as they are inclined to be communicative and talkative. They are seldom reserved and more often lack poise. They possess little tact, and their remarks are often ill-timed and indiscreet. Generally ready to talk and discuss any subject. While sincere, honest, generous, and confidential, they are apt to "gossip."

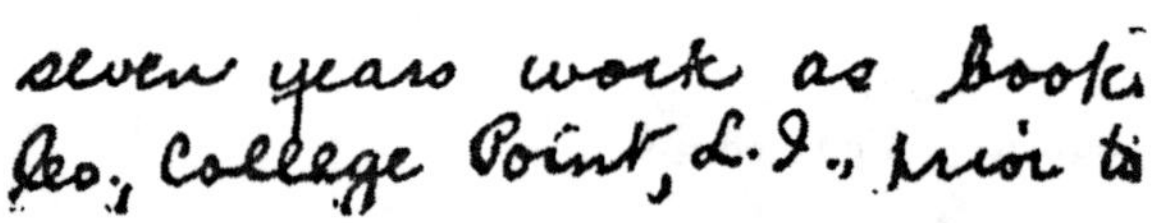

When the small letters *a, o, d,* and *g* are written with the tops closed tightly.

(The intent of the writer must be evident, to render these signs potent; the writing must be spontaneous and deliberate.)

These writers are tactful, discreet, cautious, and of reserved nature. There is always a lack of frankness; not inclined to be outspoken or to take others into their confidence. They have the desire and ability to keep their own counsel, consequently can guard a secret well. They have an impenetrable nature. Justice may be expected but not much mercy or sentiment.

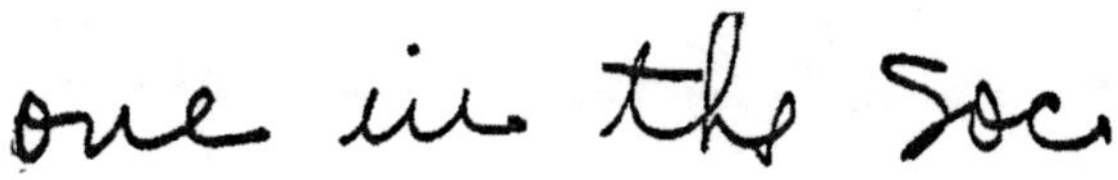

When the small letters *a*, *o*, *d*, *g* are closed *and looped* at the top.

This is a reliable sign for secretiveness and often denotes hypocrisy, which is frequently carried to the point of falsehood, if cornered. The nature is very reserved and uncommunicative; rarely talks about personal affairs; careful not to commit themselves; very difficult to draw from them an opinion on any subject.

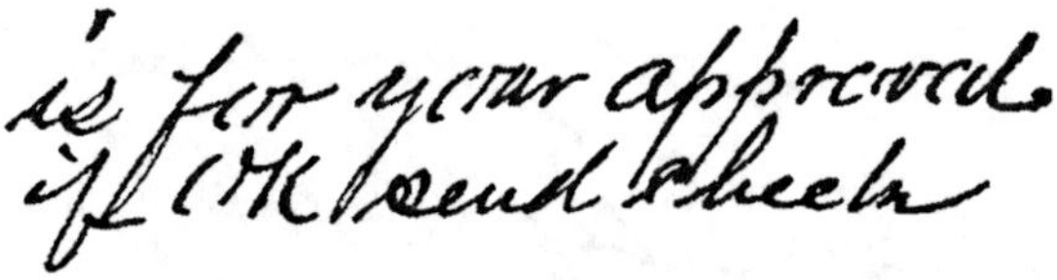

When the small letters *a*, *o*, *d*, *g* are *open* at the base.

(This manner of writing this form of *a*, *o*, *d*, *g* is always spontaneous, and it cannot be written by any one whose nature is opposed to the traits cited.)

This is a rare form and not often seen; well that it is so, for it denotes deliberate misrepresentation, dissimulation and falsehood. If the sign is repeatedly used, the nature tends to hypocrisy and dishonesty.

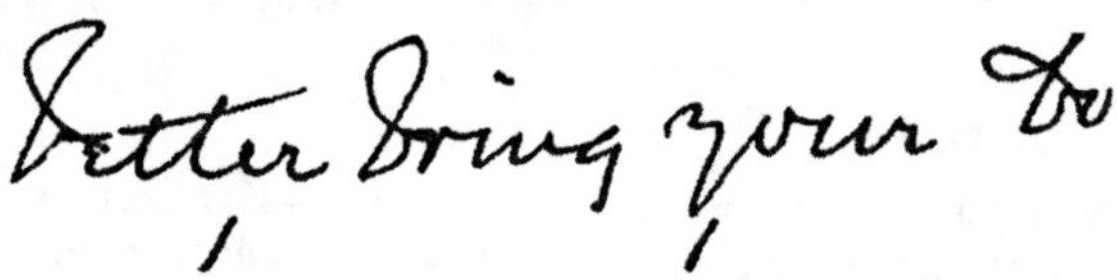

THE SMALL LETTER *b*.

When written with the *incurve*, *i.e.* the initial stroke begins at the right of the letter, swings to the left, forming a loop.

Usually an egotistical, self-appreciative, proud, and self-reliant nature.

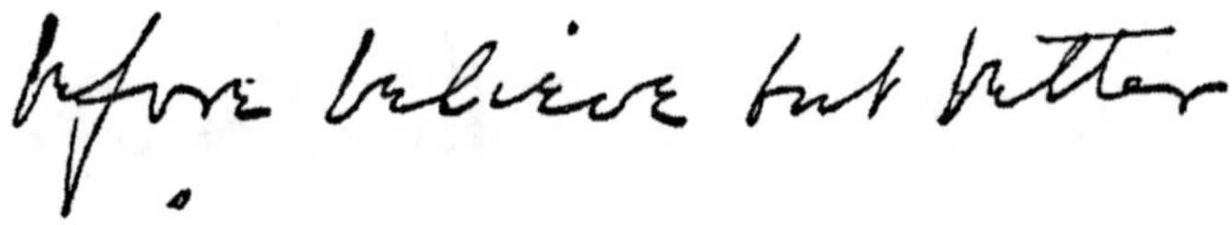

THE *b* IN *before* AND *believe*

When the small letter *b* is written with an initial down stroke made heavy, and without the loop.

Denotes conciseness with practical ideas and abilities. A distinctive individuality, with originality that is not usually commonplace. Often has strong convictions. When the initial down stroke is not heavy, these significations are modified.

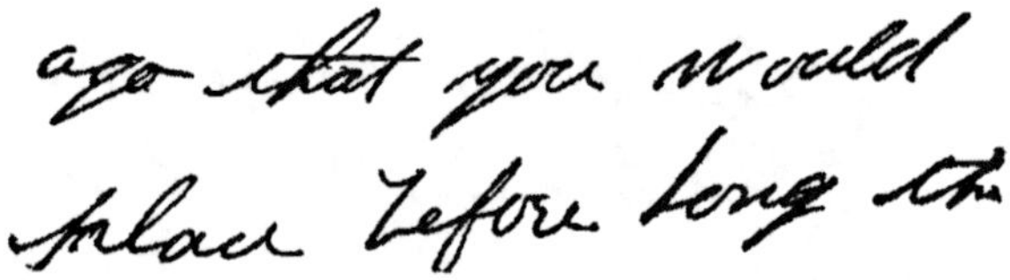

THE *b* IN *before*

When the small letter *b* is written with an initial hook, instead of the loop, before beginning the stroke.

Denotes one who is talkative and fond of conversation, chatty, with much to say. Usually a rapid and animated talker.

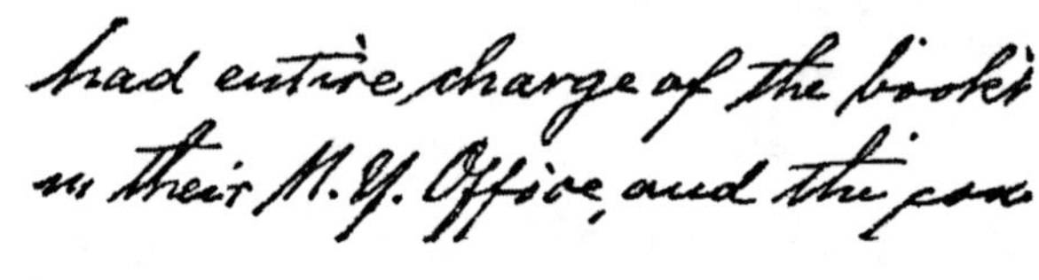

THE SMALL LETTER *d*

When the stem is written high, either as a stroke or with very slim loop.

Pride and self-respect are indicated. These writers always entertain a high regard for personal dignity, and will never submit to anything that will compromise or demean their conception of personal quality. They are retiring and self-depreciative. When other signs confirm it, a high sense of honor is noted which may be exactingly strict.

When the small letter *d* is written with a short stem, or made low down on the stem, with or without loop.

The significations for this form of *d* are almost infallible. Self-respect may not be lacking, but regard for personal dignity is less than that shown in the high stem, because the writer is willing to waive it in favor of some personal gratification or profit, considering policy of more consequence than principle. This trait seems to be put on and taken off to suit the occasion. Persons who write the low *d* stem habitually, are rather lacking in a high sense of honor, and the conscience is more pliable, because more scope for action is allowed, without fear of compromising the dignity or morals.

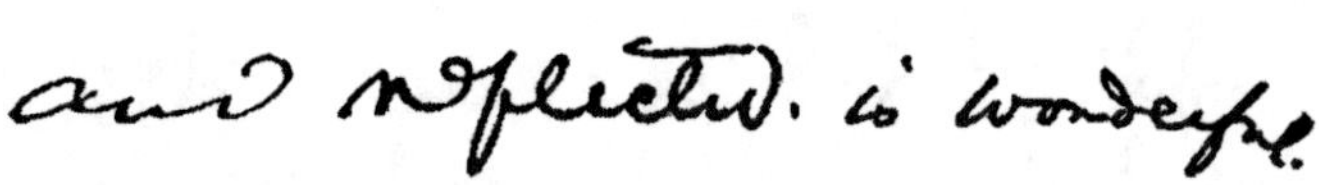

When the small letter *d* is made with its final stroke curved upward with small backward curl that joins the succeeding letter or word, or is curved upward at the end of a word. This style of the letter *d* is termed the *Greek d.*

When other signs agree, this *d* is indicative of scholarly attainments, literary discrimination, or nicety of tastes in the cultivated arts. It always indicates talent and culture, and is usually seen in the handwriting of persons of ability, or with those who are more or less accomplished in literary pursuits. It indicates fluency in writing, or one whose leanings are toward writing, either as a pastime or a profession.

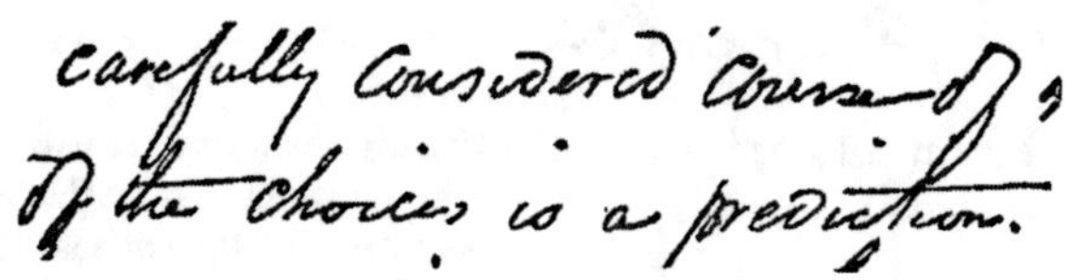

When the small letter *d* is made with the final stroke gracefully

Indicates an analytical and critical mind, which is apt to be sensitive and curved upward and back, at the end of a word. This is also a *Greek d.*

easily prejudiced; the nature is largely introspective. These writers have strong mental cultivation and powers of imagination, with an instinctive culture and keen desire for learning. When this sign is seen in crude hands, it indicates aspiration. Writers and advanced thinkers, use this form of *d.*

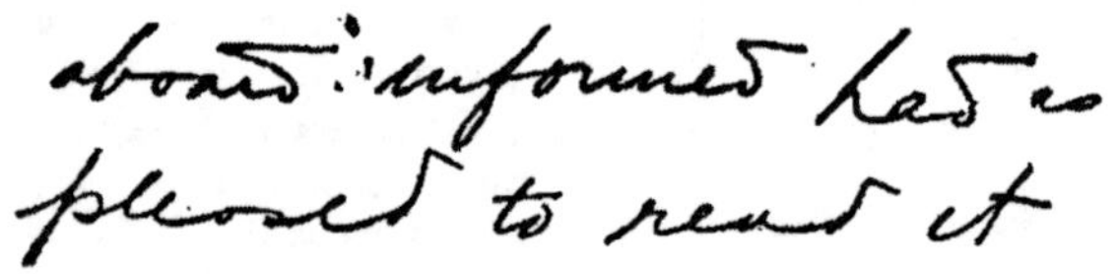

When the small letter *d* is curved upward and prominently to the right.

Inclined to be gay, fanciful, and of fun-loving nature; the tendency is to be coquettish and flirtatious. If in large or diffused hand the sign is augmented. Love of admiration and a strong desire for approval are also indicated.

When the small letter *d* is made with the final stroke curved upward and ending in a little spiral curl.

Denotes conceit, presumption, vanity, or pretension. Given to levity, with a shallow and pleasure-loving nature. An eccentric and odd manner, that betokens absentmindedness.

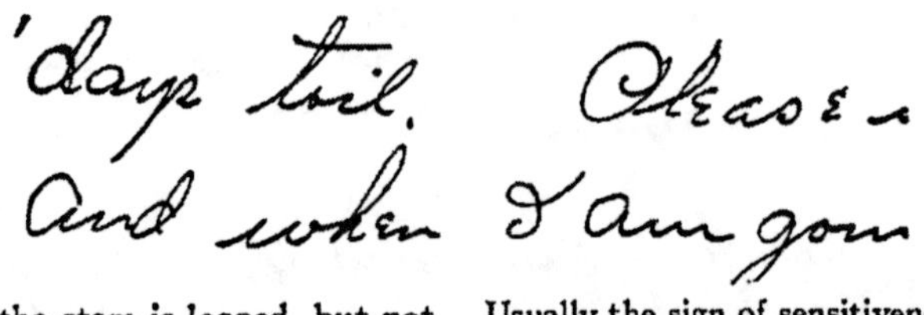

When the stem is looped, but not large or inflated.

Usually the sign of sensitiveness; pride is easily wounded and the feelings hurt, because they take offense quickly and, often at little things. It indicates a talkative and communicative nature, with some oratorical ability.

When the upper loop is inflated.

Denotes unreasonable sensitiveness and general morbidness of mind, particularly on the subject of one's pride and rights.

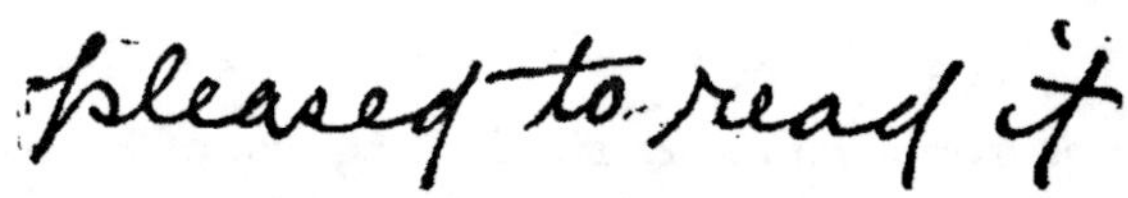

When the final stroke of the *d* extends below the line.

Denotes a person who is strongly opinionated, with decided views and strong convictions, and usually with narrow prejudices. Obstinacy is nearly always shown; will stick to an opinion.

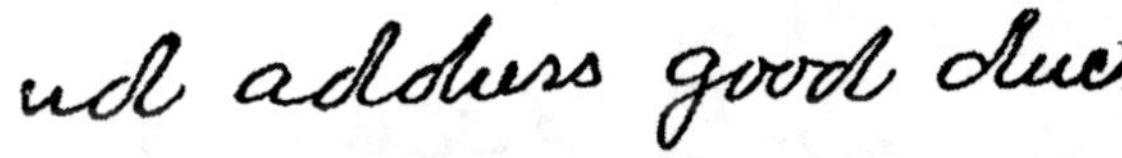

When the upstroke of the *d* is separated from the down stroke, and at the left of the stem.

The signification for this sign is taciturnity; has little to say, but may be a good listener. The writer has the ability to deceive but does not intend to do so.

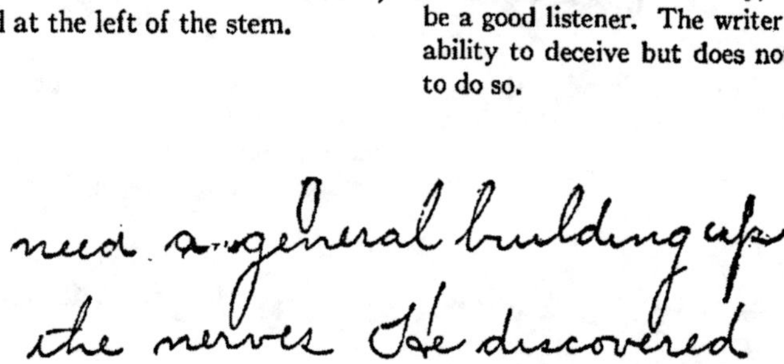

When the stem is pointed—the down stroke is retraced over the upstroke, giving the appearance of having been made with one single stroke.

The general signification for this sign is *sarcasm* but the writer may otherwise have an amiable, kindly disposition, until aroused, when the ability to say sharp and cutting things, and use sarcastic terms, becomes manifest.

THE SMALL LETTER *e*

When the small letter *e* is made in the form of the Greek character, or like the capital *E*.

Denotes a nature that is acquisitive of knowledge; desire for culture and education. This sign is frequently seen in those who are unconscious of having any such inclinations.

THE SMALL LETTER *i*

This letter is fraught with much meaning, and should be carefully considered in making an analysis, the manner of making and placing the dot being the factor. The *j* dot has the same qualities.

When the small letter *i* or *j* is undotted.

Usually a poor memory; thoughtlessness; liveliness. In most cases it indicates an untidy, heedless, slovenly person. Always denotes haste and lack of concentration.

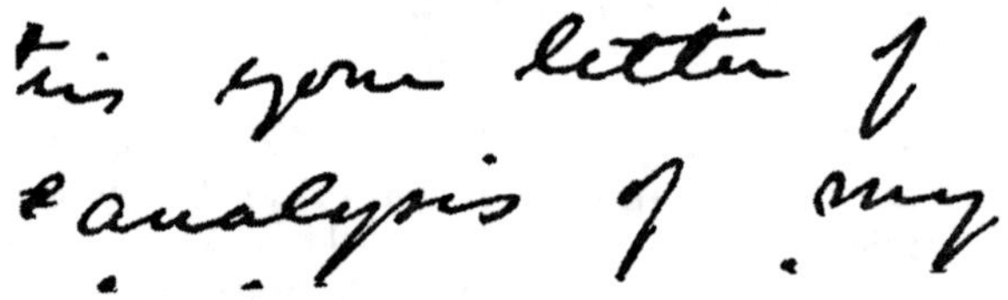

When the dot is placed at the right of the letter, not too high or too low.

Quickness, vivacity, animation, impulsiveness, and impatience. Usually an inconsiderate, ardent, happy-go-lucky nature, wanting forethought.

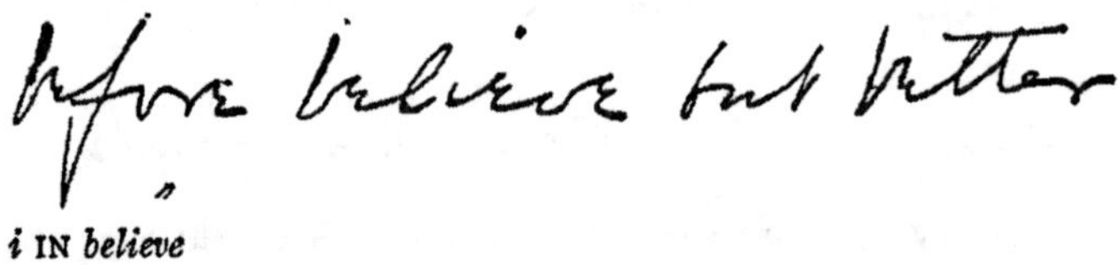

THE *i* IN *believe*

When the dot is placed high and to the right of the letter.

Impulsiveness, generosity, and aspiration with active imagination. Enthusiasm, enterprise, and curiosity are displayed.

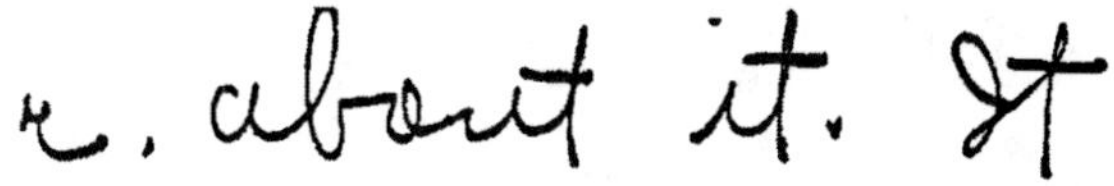

When the dot is placed to the left, or over the letter, but not close to the stem.

Denotes deliberation and slowness, with the tendency toward procrastination. This sign is not, however, as reliable as the *t* crossing to the left. Usually difficult to make up the mind on any undertaking, or to carry out a purpose. These writers lack steadfastness and continuity of thought. Mind and actions do not always work in harmony. An apprehensive, over-careful, and nervous disposition.

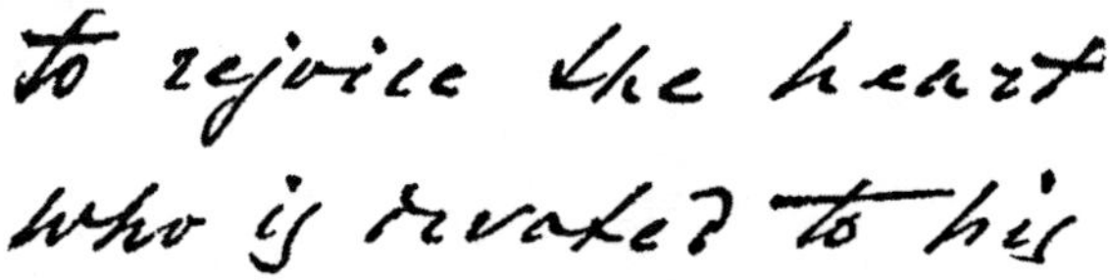

When the dot is placed close to the letter.

A retentive memory. Carefulness, caution, and lack of imagination. Attention to details; reflection and good judgment. Seldom carried away by enthusiasm or hero worship; rarely romantic or visionary. Powers of mental concentration strong; the capacity for protracted attention and study in some one direction. Exactness.

When the dot is made lightly, but firmly.

If other signs confirm it, the indication is moral courage. These writers dare to do what they believe is right, without fear of criticism or of the consequences.

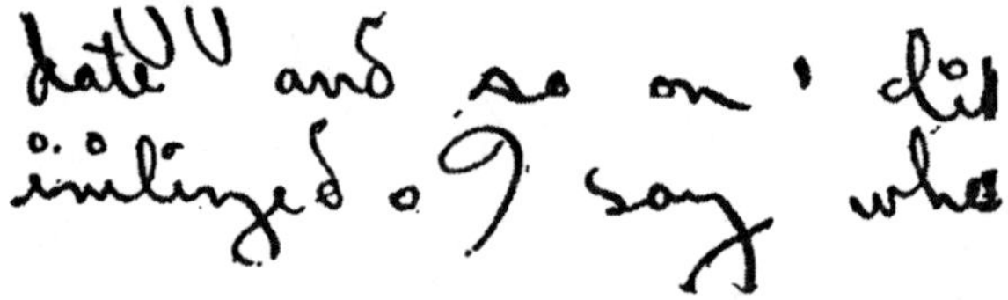

When small circles are used in place of dots.

The sign may be attributed to threatened mental disturbance or ignorant eccentricity. In cases of suspected mental disturbance the writing will be individual and well balanced, the circles supplying the first hint of derangement. Used as an eccentric fad, the habit will pass off as soon as the writer develops in mental strength, and assumes responsibilities that compel him to relinquish faddish notions.

When the dots are made large and heavy.

Materialism, or a nature yearning for worldly pleasures and enjoyments. When extremely large and heavy, it indicates an ungovernable temper, with strong passions, if not an absolutely brutal tendency. The nature is usually assertive.

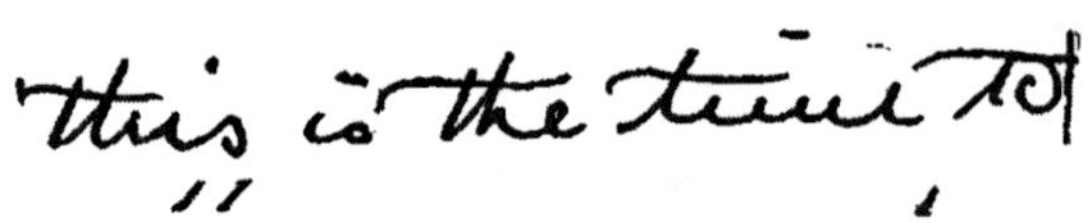

When dots are made like horizontal dashes.

The indications are an energetic lively nature.

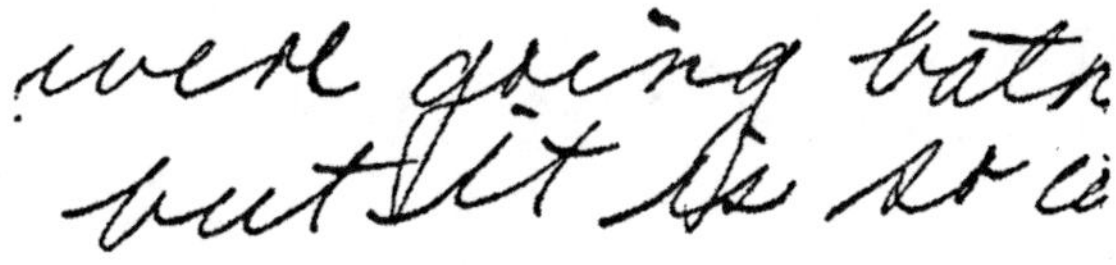

When the dots are made like descending dashes. — Opinionativeness and physical courage are indicated.

When dots are made like wavy dashes. — Love of fun, and humor; a light-hearted nature, with slight inconstancy.

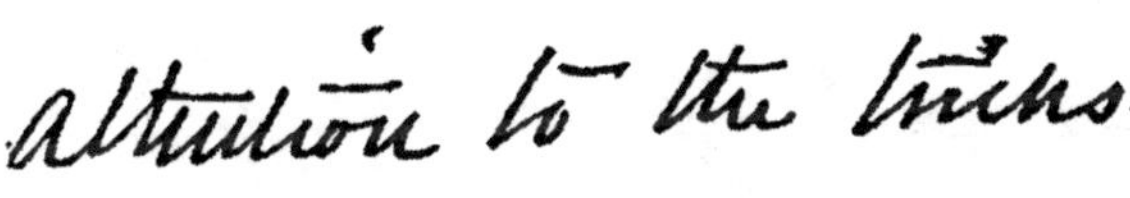

When dots are angular and irregular in form, at times a dot; at other times a dash; now and then curved or straight dashes. — Irritability and more or less excitable temperament.

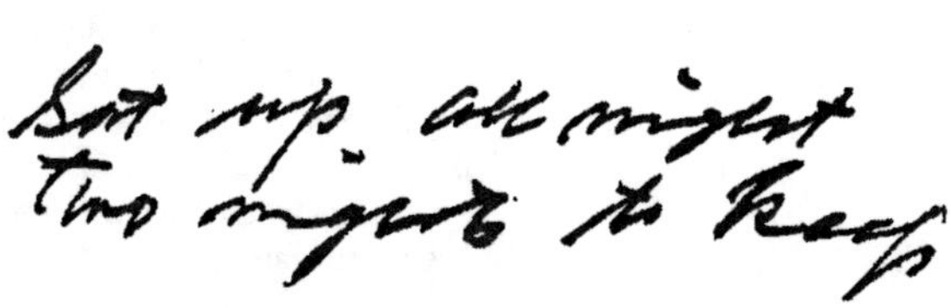

When the dot is made club shape. — Brutal potentialities are indicated, with an active and materialistic mentality, tending to what is coarse and sensual.

THE SMALL LETTERS *m* AND *n*

When these letters are written like the small letters *w* and *u*, in the concaved form, or *abducent* writing.

Adaptability, suavity, kindliness, and a good mixer. Usually alert and quick to grasp problems.

When these letters are written in the conventional form with the tops *rounded—the adducent form.*

An unadaptable, simple, but honest nature. Usually in the industrial class, as mechanic or tradesman. Few holding clerkships write this style of hand.

THE SMALL LETTER *p*

When the lower loop of the small letter *p* is made long, and sweeps well up on the left of the letter.

Physical agility, love of exercise, of athletics, and of all outdoor sports and recreations appeal. Usually of good muscular development, they make good dancers; sports of all kinds, calling for physical exercise are attractive. Art and poetry, with musical tastes, are highly developed. When the lower part of this letter is made in the form of a stroke, instead of loop, the above signs are accentuated.

When the stroke or loop of the small letter *p* is made long above, and short below, the line.

It indicates physical weakness, due to advanced years, infirmity, or mental lack of vigor, but it is not indicative of physical illness.

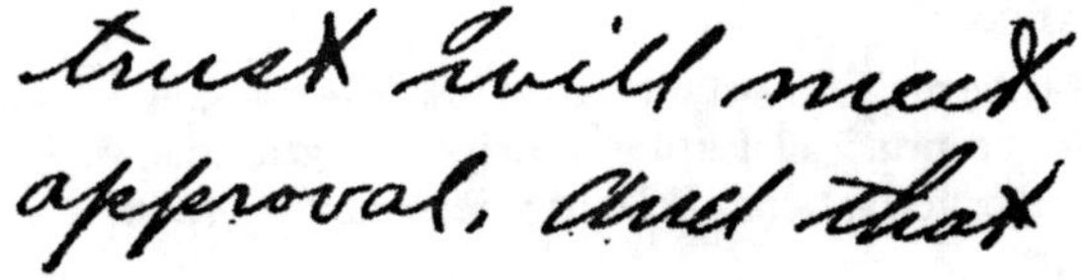

When the letter *p* is made with the lower point sharp and the upstroke ascends on the right of the stem.

The general signification for this sign is aggressiveness and sometimes initiativeness.

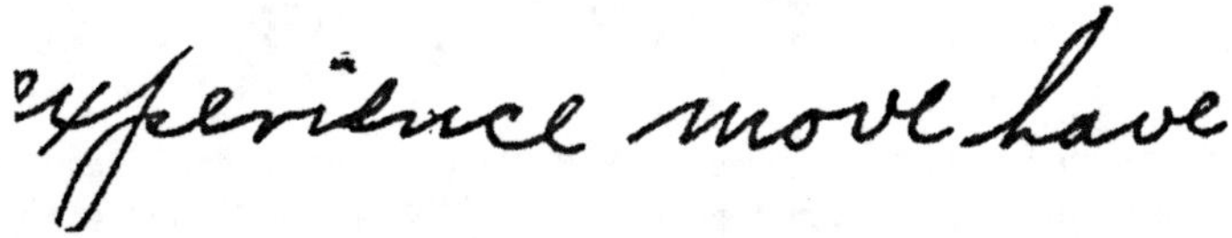

When the stroke or loop is made short above and long below the line.

Indicates muscularity.

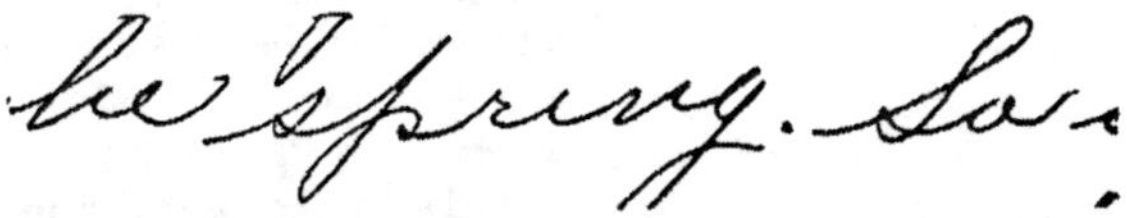

When the lower point is not sharp and ascends upward on the left of the letter.

A peace-loving disposition.

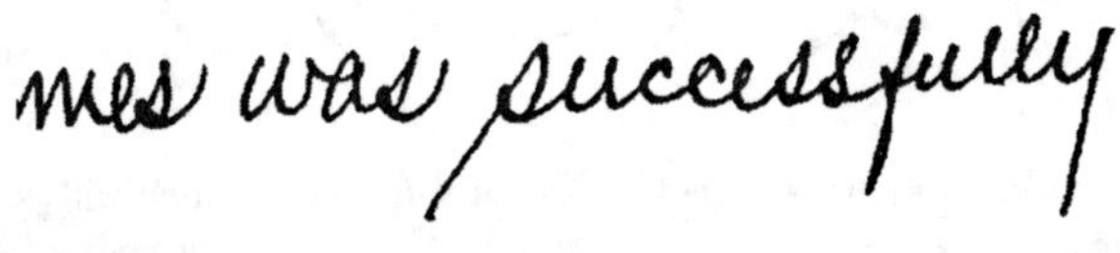

THE SMALL LETTER *s*

When the small letter *s* is closed with a loop, as if tied in a knot to the upstroke.

Some authors insist that this sign indicates lack of candor, and a disposition to dodge the truth on occasion; that they are persons whose assertions must be accepted with allowance; rarely can be depended upon for frankness and are not always straight-forward in business dealings. (The author of this work has been able, on many occasions, to confirm this sign, but holds to the opinion that it is not a reliable sign, unless the text furnishes additional evidence to support it.)

THE SMALL LETTER *t*

This is one of the most important letters in the list of graphological signs. The *t* bar is the principal feature, and its strength, manner of crossing, length, and other formations of the bar, determine its value.

When the stem is carefully crossed. This means that the bar is neither on the right nor on the left of the stem, but carefully set across it.

When the *t* bar shows that it has been deliberately placed on the stem, without dash or haste, it denotes a careful and painstaking person, with good will-power and constancy of purpose. It denotes a calm, sure, certain, even character, with good determination and executive ability in a trained hand. In the untutored hand it denotes moderation and, probably, mediocrity, but always conscientiousness with more or less deliberation and firmness.

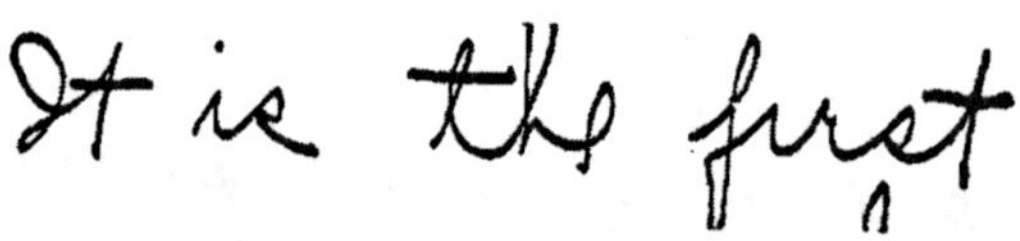

When the *t* is heavily crossed, usually across the stem.

Denotes firmness, much will power, determination and aggressiveness, with assurance and self-reliance. Force of energy, physical courage, daring and persistence of effort are indicated. When the bar is long and the crossing is heavy much assertiveness and often a defiant air in manner are shown.

When the *t* is weakly crossed, meaning that it is carelessly made,

Denotes lack of strong will power. Usually without much force of char-

with a thin, listless stroke whether, across the stem or above it or to the right or left of the stem.

acter, and lacks firmness and decision. Writer is not likely to be steadfast in aims and purposes, and may be easily dissuaded; the nature is vascillating and irresolute. Often has mediocre and commonplace capabilities.

When the *t* bar is placed to the right of the stem (weak strokes are rarely made to the right of the stem.)

Impulsiveness, quickness, animation, and hastiness. When bar flies off from right of the letter without touching it, it usually signifies impatience. The initiative faculty is present in a corresponding degree, with enterprise, enthusiasm, curiosity, and ambition always indicated.

When the *t* is crossed to the right, in the angular hand.

Denotes a quick temper; intolerant of reproof or restraint. Often these writers are nervous and irritable; remarks are stinging, when angered or annoyed.

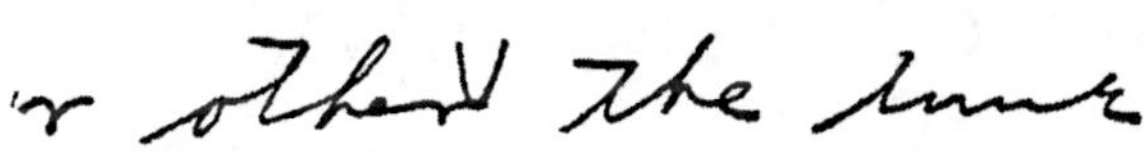

When the *t* is crossed to the left of the stem.

This is the infallible sign for procrastination. The habit of putting off. Cannot be depended upon to fulfill promises, however well intentioned. A slow, hesitating, cautious nature. These persons may be extremely active, and appear to be busy all the time, and probably are, but they accomplish little in the long run because of this lack of decisiveness and putting-off habit.

When the *t* bar ascends.	One who is hopeful but inclined to be imaginative and fanciful. Generally ambitious with many irons in the fire. Apt to take an optimistic view of things. When the bar is very ascending, imitation and mimicry.

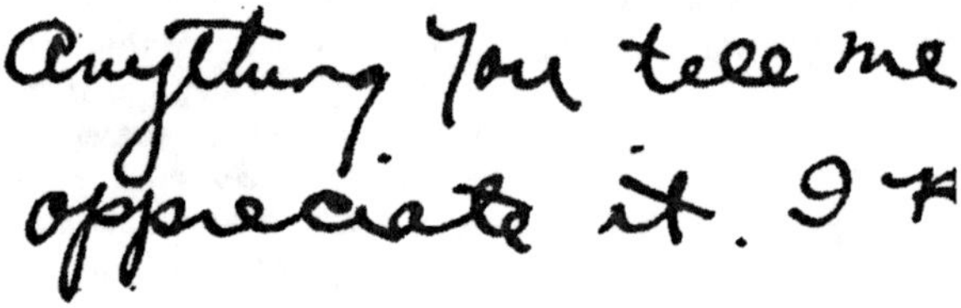

When the *t* bar descends.	Usually an unambitious nature. Apt to be obstinate and self-willed. When very much downward, great perseverance and misdirected energy; apt to persevere when good sense would direct one to desist. Likely to be pessimistic and opinionated.

When the final stroke of the stem extends below the line.	The writer has decided views on many subjects and strong convictions, with usually narrow prejudices.

When the *t* crossing is made in the form of a triangle.	Always sensitive; a conceited and egotistical nature, which carries with it a certain reservedness.

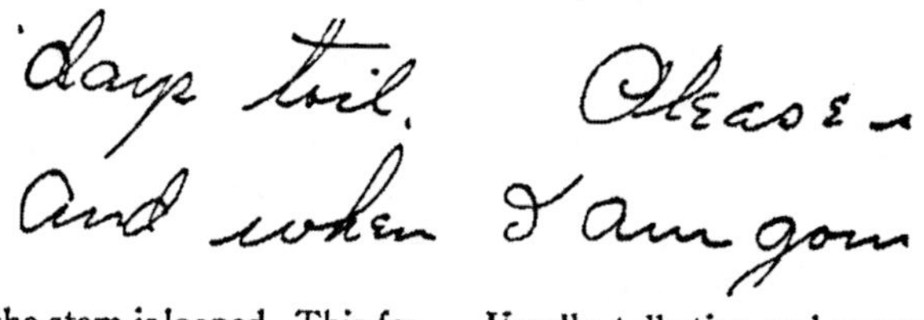

When the stem is looped. This feature applies also to the small letter *d*. See *t* in *toil*.

Usually talkative and communicative. A sensitive pride, which makes one quick to resent any reflection upon personal conduct; takes offense too readily. Often a shallow intellect.

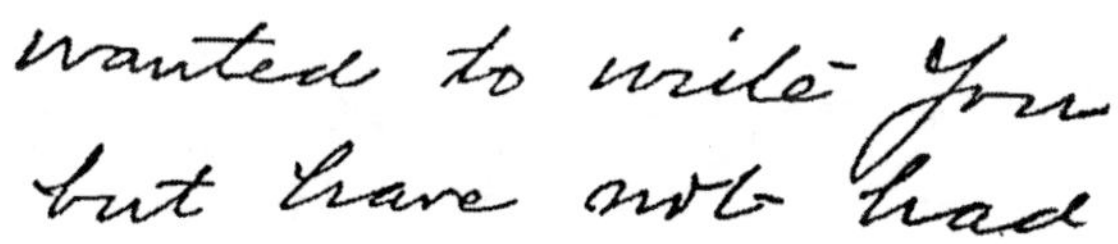

When the *t* stem is made pointed; no loops.

Writers of this style of *t* are reserved and dignified.

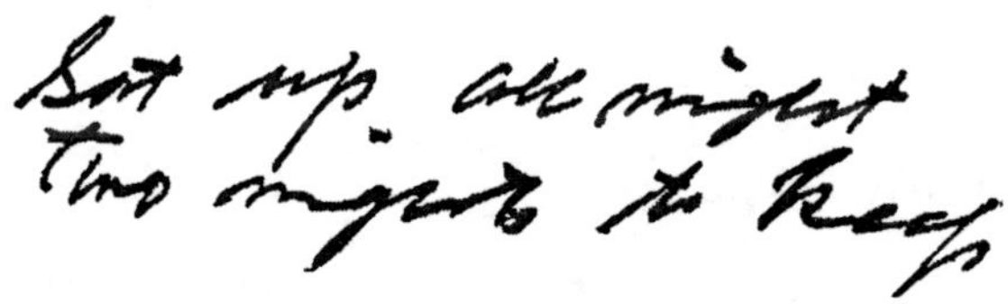

When the stem is opened at the bottom, like an inverted *V*.

Deception and evasion, not always intentional.

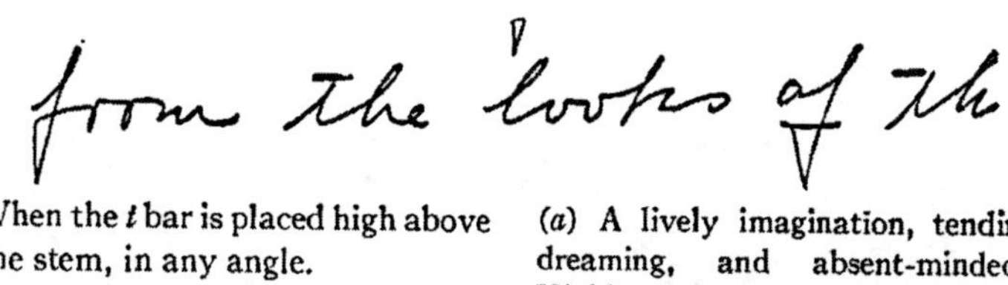

When the *t* bar is placed high above the stem, in any angle.

(*a*) A lively imagination, tending to dreaming, and absent-mindedness. Highly aspirational and visionary. A builder of air-castles. (*b*) Perseverance, resistance, and love of authority indicated. (*c*) When in commonplace writing, a conventional nature with prejudices.

When the *t* stem is left uncrossed, without the bar.

Lack of retentive memory. An acquiescent nature, lacking force of character; little, if any, resistance power. Usually lack of purpose or determination.

When the stem is sometimes uncrossed, and at other times crossed.

An irresolute, vascillating nature, with an undecided disposition.

When the stem is uncrossed, but is finished with an angular final upstroke.

Lack of initiative and will power and some obstinacy.

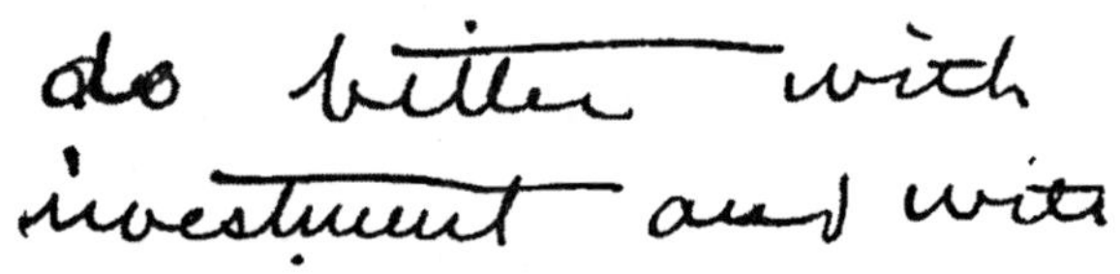

When the *t* bar is irregular in shape.

A capricious, volatile, unstable character, hardly to be depended upon.

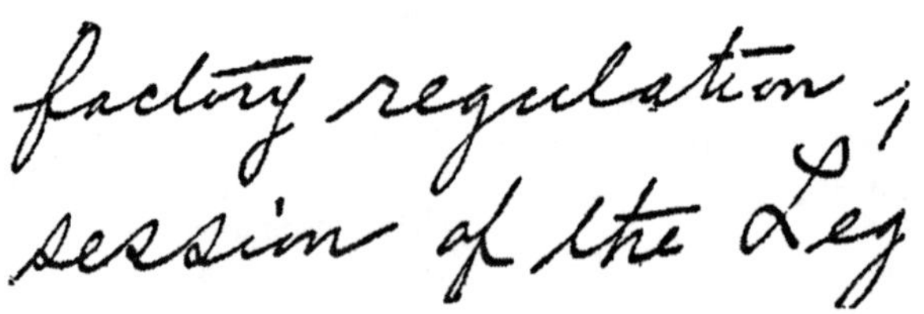

When the bar is uniformly thick and regular.

Thoughtful and serious turn of mind. Quiet decision, calmness, composure, temperate nature.

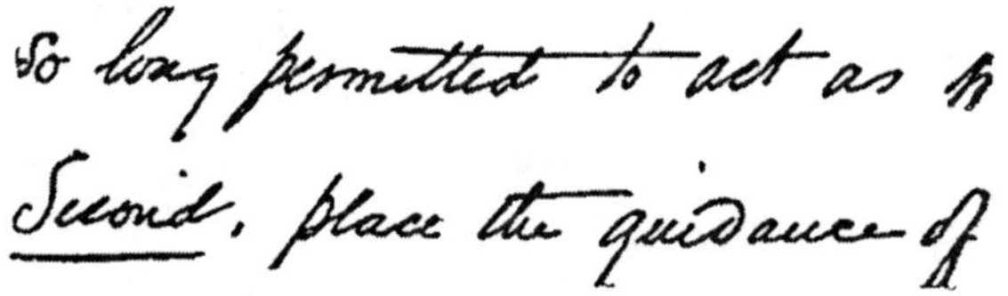

When the bar is long, fine, and of equal thickness throughout. | Energy, ardor, ambition.

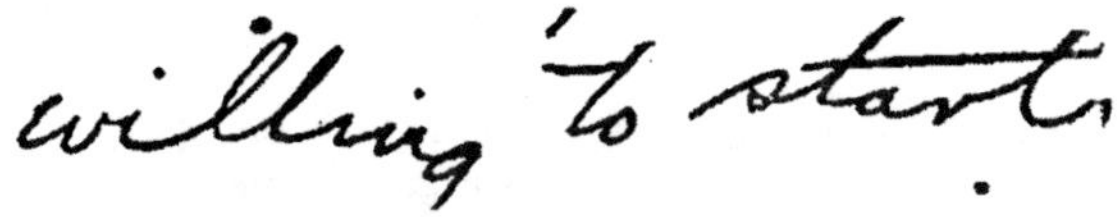

When the bar is long and crosses two or three letters. | Impulsiveness; an unobservant nature.

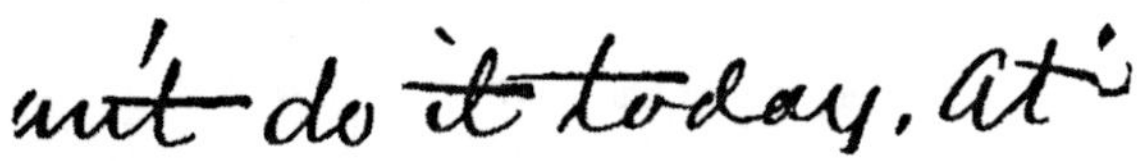

When the bar is long, thicker at finish than at start, and crushed down on the other letters. | Arbitrary will.

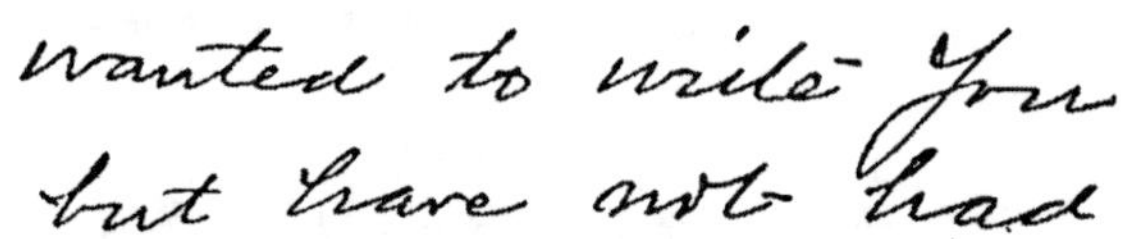

When the bar is sometimes long, other times short, now and again a mere dot. | Imagination, fantasy. Music composers frequently use this form of *t* crossing.

(A well known pianist and writer of musical compositions.)

When the bar flies into the letters of the next word. | Animation, impulse, vivacity, sequence of ideas, and a jovial nature.

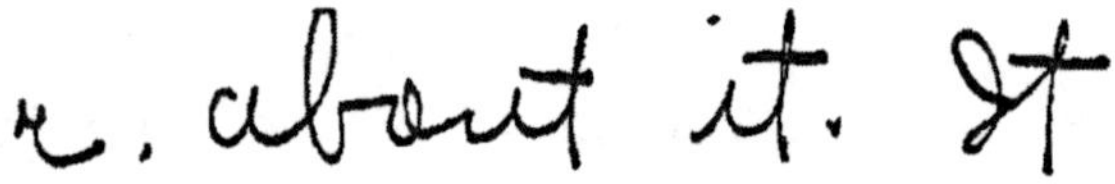

When the bar is stronger and thicker than the down stroke.	Great determination and strong will.

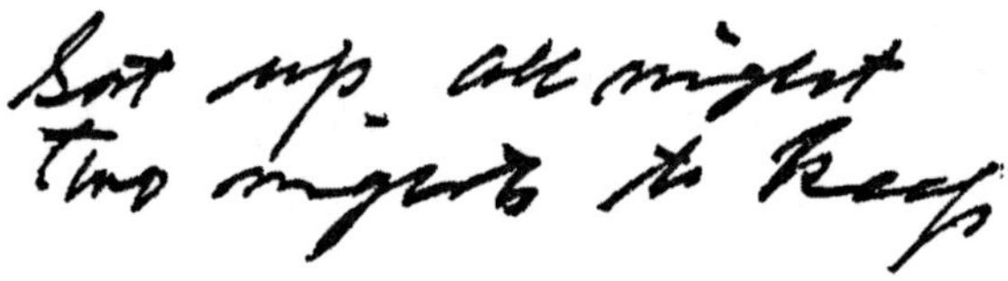

When the bar is short and thick and crushed down on the stem.	Contrariness of thought, action, and strength of mind.

When the bar is very long and strong.	Indicates will power.

When the bar is club shaped.	Brutality and inconsiderateness shown.

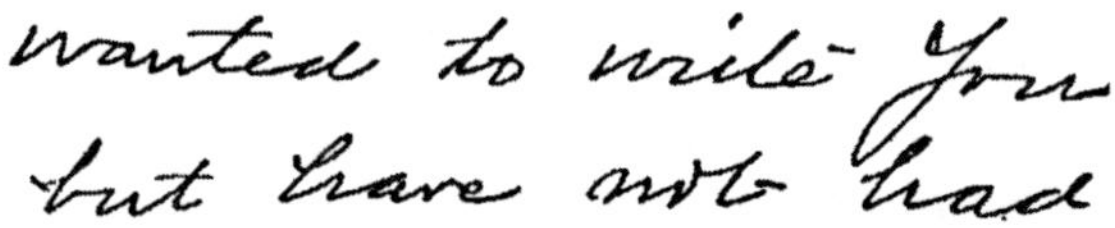

When the bar is light and short.	Nature is easily imposed upon.

When the bar is spear shaped.	Inclined to be sharp and sarcastic in speech.

When the bar is curved like a bow with the ends *downward*.

A change in the impulses and passions that were once strong, now checked and under control.

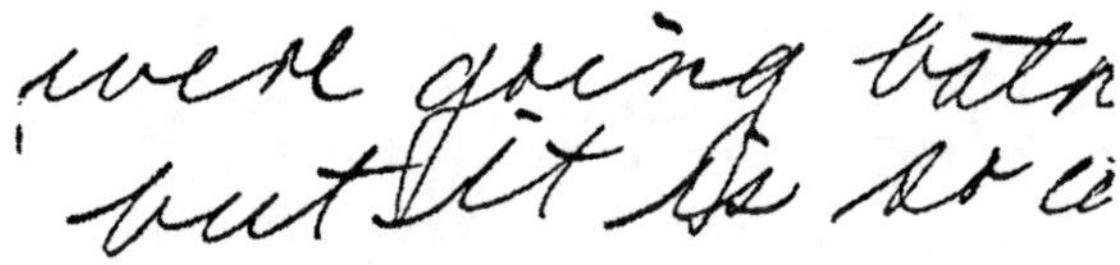

When the bar is curved like a bow, with the ends *upward*.

Of shallow nature, too emotional, and of yielding disposition.

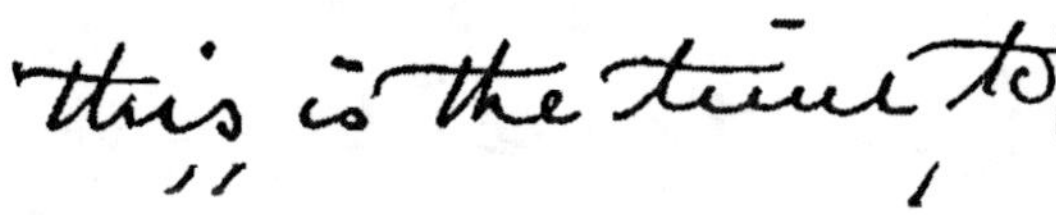

When the bar is wavy.

Fun, humor, jolly disposition, but inconstancy in affection.

When the bar is short and arrow-like.

Domineering, satirical, and critical nature.

When the bar is dot-like and extremely short.

The power of observation with the faculty of seeing appreciatively.

When the bar is curved at either end and scroll shaped.	Denotes a light mentality.

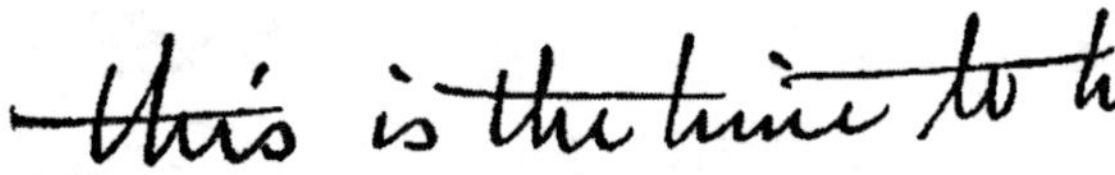

When the bar is long and pointed at its finish.	Signifies meanness, malice, and anger.

When the bar is made with a tiny hook at its finish.	Tenacity of purpose and firmness.

When the bar is made in the form of a lash or whip.	Effusiveness and fancy.

When the bar is flourished.	Imagination, pretension, egotism.

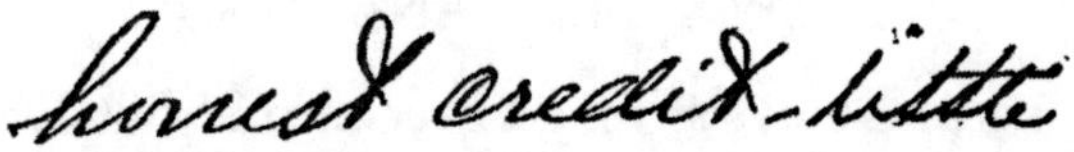

When the bar is substituted by a looped triangle low down on the stem.

Persistency is always shown in one form or another.

A SPECIMEN ANALYSIS

In making an analysis from a specimen of handwriting, the student should make notes of the signs in the script, and jot them down with their meanings. Having completed the list of signs, arrange them in the order of their classification, as indicated in the *Elements of Graphology*, which, as previously stated, should be memorized, precisely for the reasons now being discussed. The first of these elements is *style*, the second is *slope*, etc., etc. Continue in this manner throughout the entire specimen, until all the features have been *dissected* and their meanings applied. You are now ready to delineate the letter, which you do by neutralizing the signs, grouping the characteristics that are similar, or combining related traits of character, for the double purpose of making the delineation accurate and to prevent verbosity.

This plan of separating the signs, and giving them their meanings, and arranging them in classified order, insures accuracy, and prevents too much dependence on the memory, for the best of us are not too well equipped with unfailing memory, at least, until we have become thoroughly familiar with the signs and their order of procedure, and have had experience enough to trust the memory. Skilled graphologists become adept in *reading* the signs, and may not always need these preliminary memoranda, unless a record of the script is desired for filing away for future reference.

Unless some standard form of a record sheet is employed, the student will be required to make this record every time he analyzes a specimen. This entails much time and labor. On page 122 will be found a specimen record form, similar to that used by the author for several years, in his professional work, and which has proved its utility as a permanent record of the specimen analyzed, to which frequent reference was often required to ascertain change of character in applicants who have held positions one year or more with the same firm.

CHARLES E. FRANCIS
ATTORNEY AND COUNSELLOR AT LAW
150 NASSAU STREET
MANHATTAN NEW YORK CITY

TELEPHONE CONNECTION

June 16, 1919.

My dear Mr. Smith:

I have long been interested in your graphological researches and having tested your apparent knowledge thereof, from time to time, have been amazed at the revelations

Surely the time must come when as an exact science it will become admissable in our Courts as competent evidence

Hoping you will persist until you have realized a great financial success I am

Yours faithfully

C. E. Francis

This record form may be had in printed sheets, of convenient size, containing all the classifications, in consecutive order, by which the student may record any specimen of handwriting, and use it as a working sheet, and also for filing away for future reference. These record forms are put up in pads containing 100 sheets, and the cost is *nominal.* These pads may be obtained from the Gregg Publishing Company.

A SPECIMEN ANALYZED

In order to give the student a practical example of the method of making an analysis, and of writing a delineation from the analysis, the following illustration is presented. A few lines of the first page and a few lines of the last page, with signature, are given; in every other respect the specimen is intact and in the original size.

This writer possesses a keen intellect with an amiable disposition and fun-loving nature. He is bubbling over with levity and good nature. (Abducent writing, wavy *t-bars* shown in the crossing of the *t's* in *Smith*, in *time*, in *exact*, in *competent* and in *great.*) The power of observation with the faculty of seeing appreciatively are strongly marked. (t-bars are extremely short.) Impulses and emotions, however, are under control, although the nature is unambitious, due to pessimistic and opinionated tendencies. (An occasional *descending t-bar*, others curved like a bow with the ends downward, the first t-crossing in *interested* on the first line; *t* in *it* on the seventh line and in *persist* on the tenth line. The script denotes a nature that is acquisitive of knowledge, with keen desire for culture and what is refined and proper. (Persistent use of the Greek *e* and *d*, modified by the occasional ending of the *d stroke* in a spiral curl, which indicates a too pleasure-loving nature; some vanity and coquetry.) Business instinct is strongly indicated as well as enterprise and organization ability with a vivid imagination, that renders him resourceful and quick to see an advantage. Loop letters are well developed above and below the line, those below line being especially so.

His instinctive mind, modified by rare deductive powers denotes one having patience, and capable of self-control, particularly so under trying circumstances, as in debate and in heated arguments when his versatility becomes manifest. (The equal use of *disconnected* and *connected* letters, the absence of *initial* strokes, the closed *a* and *o*, and the generally firm *t* crossings.) Judgment of matters and people are dictated by an inner consciousness, for he is quick of comprehension, critical, analytical and is usually a good judge of character.

Tact and a reserved, conservative, discreet nature are shown, with a well-ordered mind. He rarely acts hastily in matters of business and never becomes confused or excited; these are the attributes of an astute and judicial mind. (Closed *a* and *o*, well-spaced writing, straight base lines, pointed tops of letters and large lower loops.)

His fun-loving nature is so strongly marked that he often misses opportunities for substantial advancement, when his light-heartedness and high perception of things beautiful tend to sway his otherwise staid demeanor. His artistic tastes are highly developed and, if cultivated, would prove pleasing and attractive as a pastime or a business venture. (The tendency to *ornate* writing, shown in the capital *M* in *My* and *Mr.* and the graceful formation of his signature.) The signs, however, indicate a bit of egotism and mild conceit, with marked desire for approbation, weaknesses that are pardonable in a character so full of achievement.

The total absence of shading in any of the down strokes is indicative of quiet, modest tastes with tendencies to a complaisant and simple disposition, with delicate sensibilities, temperate habits, and an unobtrusive manner. A high sense of honor and kindly consideration for others are characteristic.

The student may proceed in this manner, until all traits or propensities have been noted, excluding of course the technical references printed in italics, which are written here for his benefit, showing the features to which the interpretations refer.

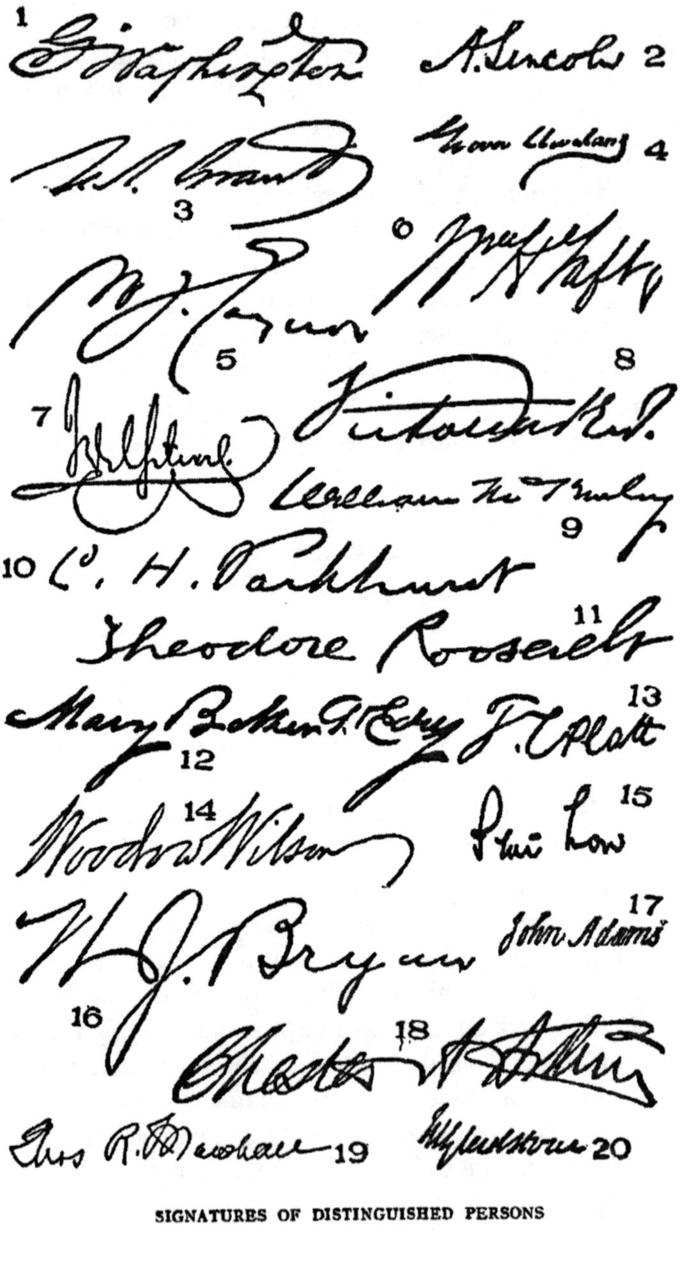

SIGNATURES OF DISTINGUISHED PERSONS

SIGNATURES OF DISTINGUISHED PERSONS

The following is the key to the Signatures of Distinguished persons appearing on the preceding page. The interpretations were deduced from the chirographic signs displayed in each specimen, and according to the rules of graphology, and not from what the author may know of these personages from historical knowledge. Broad-minded and truly great men write plain signatures; this reveals their characters.

No. 1	George Washington	An intuitive mind; sociable and humorous.
No. 2	A. Lincoln	A keen intellect; resourceful.
No. 3	U. S. Grant	Virility; energy; protectiveness.
No. 4	Grover Cleveland	Keen, concentrative mind.
No. 5	W. J. Gaynor	Highly developed mentality; irritability.
No. 6	Wm. H. Taft	Refined; whole-souled; hearty; jovial.
No. 7	Ex-Emperor William	Intriguing nature; arrogant; self-laudatory.
No. 8	Queen Victoria	Arbitrary will; impulsive.
No. 9	William McKinley	Will power; deep thinker.
No. 10	C. H. Parkhurst	Logical reasoner; studious; ambitious.
No. 11	Theodore Roosevelt	Determination; resoluteness.
No. 12	Mary Baker G. Eddy	Will power; logical thinker.
No. 13	T. C. Platt	Ambitious; acquisitive.
No. 14	Woodrow Wilson	Clearness of perception; diplomatic.
No. 15	Seth Low	Dignified, courteous, charming disposition.
No. 16	W. J. Bryan	Intuitive; indiscreet; venturesome; selfish.
No. 17	John Adams	Calm, deliberate judgment.
No. 18	Chester A. Arthur	Introspective; self-centered.
No. 19	Thos. R. Marshall	Sensitive; jovial nature; simple tastes.
No. 20	W. E. Gladstone	Brusqueness; severity; justice.

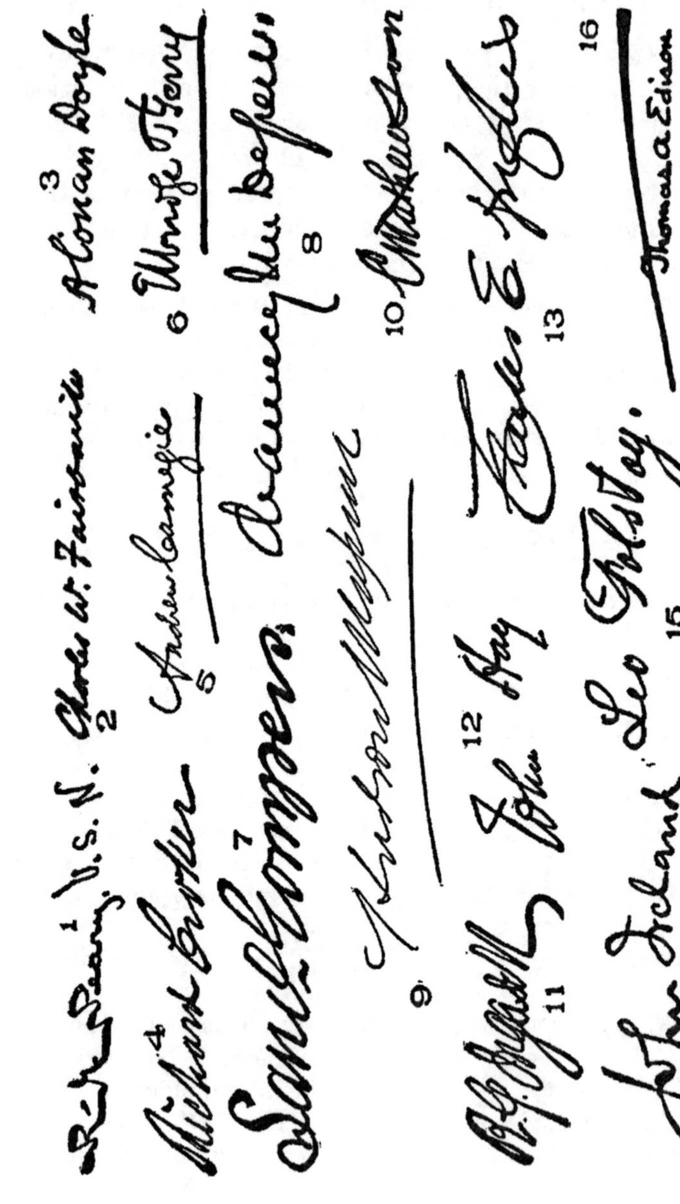

MEN MORE OR LESS IN THE PUBLIC EYE

MEN MORE OR LESS IN THE PUBLIC EYE

1. R. E. PEARY, U. S. N.	Masterful; self-reliant; marked ability.
2. CHARLES W. FAIRBANKS	Quiet and modest tastes; complaisant nature; temperate habits.
3. A. CONAN DOYLE	Excessive calculation; solicitude and extreme forethought; inquisitiveness.
4. RICHARD CROKER	Assertiveness; physical courage with material likes and dislikes; opinionated, with strong convictions.
5. ANDREW CARNEGIE	Quick and ready mind; self-confidence and self-reliance; deep thinker; brusque but honest.
6. ELBRIDGE T. GERRY	Resourceful, masterful, quick thinker; leans to the material; not spiritual.
7. SAML. GOMPERS	Delicate sensibilities; cautious; prudent.
8. CHAUNCEY M. DEPEW	Sensitive nature; cautious; prudent; a logician and investigator; mirthful.
9. HUDSON MAXIM	Highly developed sense of proportion, harmony, and adjustment.
10. C. MATTHEWSON	Great determination and resistance power; perseverance; opinionated.
11. R. G. INGERSOLL	A restless and unsettled disposition; intellect is warped.
12. JOHN HAY	Broad visioned; ambitious; forceful and strong personality.
13. CHARLES E. HUGHES	Quick and ready speaker and thinker.
14. JOHN IRELAND	An indecisive nature, lacking power for expansion, yet endowed with an open mind.
15. LEO TOLSTOY	An inspirational, psychic mind, fraught with benevolence and kindness. Very broad intellect.
16. THOMAS A. EDISON	Equipoise; the creative, constructive mind; simple tastes and desires.

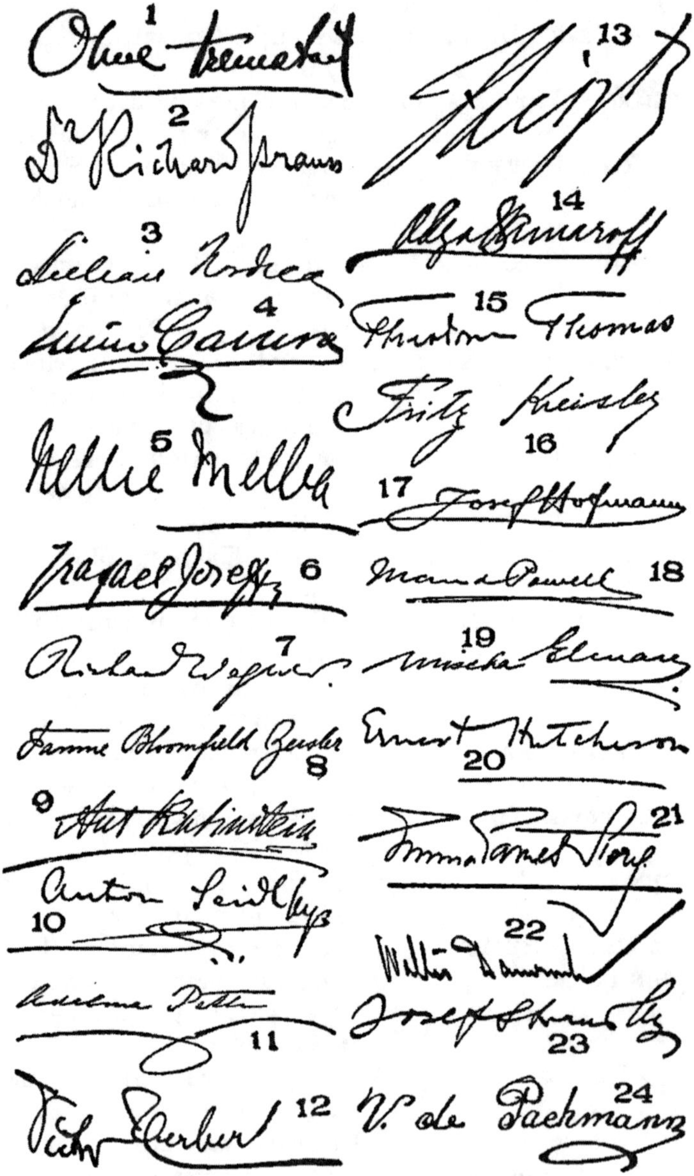

SIGNATURES OF MUSICAL CELEBRITIES

SIGNATURES OF MUSICAL CELEBRITIES

The autographs of individuals shown in this work are not displayed wholly for the interest that is attached to distinguished characters, but they are included as a means for demonstrating the psychology of environmental influences on the human intellect as a developer of habit.

The signatures printed on the preceding page are musical celebrities gathered from the four quarters of the globe. Each is imbued with the same spirit of "tone expression" that is characteristic of musical geniuses the world over. This is conclusive evidence that music is an outpouring of the soul, an inspirational instinct that cannot be otherwise than a sublime impression of mind.

Notwithstanding the similarity in musical instinct, all these distinguished persons possess different temperaments. While this similarity of musical expression is shown in the several specimens there are no two alike. This suggests that habit controls the character which is expressed in handwriting, precisely the same as one's personality controls speech.

These expressions occur in every individual whose mind has been trained to think. The higher the intellectuality the more prominent the signs. The physician thinks along physiological lines; the lawyer, along judicial lines; the theologician, along spiritual, etc. These concentrations of mind create habit; habit makes character. Persons with musical talents, particularly when highly developed, become inoculated with the spirit of rhythm, tone, and harmony. It is natural for their impressions to be reflected in their handwriting, because this outward manifestation of individuality is controlled by the emotions, and every emotion finds some form of expression in writing.

It is interesting to observe the receptivity of mind of public entertainers. When the plaudits are spontaneous and prolonged, the performer is enthused to higher and better effort. The sensitiveness and superstitions of theatrical folk are proverbial; adverse criticism or luke-warm recognition of their offering results in despair and complete mental collapse. Professional entertainers are overwhelmingly conceited and impressional; they seek and expect to receive applause, for they love to be admired and acclaimed. Approbation is their mental food.

No. 1. OLIVE FREMSTAD. Great tenacity of purpose; a bit stubborn, and an aggressive nature; moral courage and refinement; sensuously musical.

No. 2. Dr. RICHARD STRAUSS. Inspirational; resourceful with practical ideas; simple in habits; indifferent to luxury; good business instincts; tune and harmony strongly indicated.

No. 3. LILLIAN NORDICA. An acute mind; fine literary discrimination; culture and refinement clearly indicated; sensuously musical.

No. 4. ENRICO CARUSO. A complaisant nature; love of admiration and approbation; tends to the material rather than the spiritual; the musical score is very high.

No. 5. NELLIE MELBA. Morally courageous; sensitive and jealous; prudence with a sense of reputation and character that is upheld at all costs; musical tastes highly developed.

No. 6. RAPHAEL JOSEFFY. Resolution; firmness with conservation of ideas; imaginative and idealistic; animalistic nature; musical tastes highly developed.

No. 7. RICHARD WAGNER. Keen sense of the spiritual; creative, imaginative, and inspirational; musical sense strong.

No. 8. FANNIE BLOOMFIELD ZEISLER. Calm, deliberate nature; physically active, with good business instincts; rhythm and harmony highly developed.

No. 9. ANTON RUBENSTEIN. An acute mind with strong prejudices; apt to be erratic and whimsical; self-glorification and pride; intense musical feeling that is almost sensuous.

No. 10. ANTON SEIDL. Masterful; keen and deductive mind; instinctively careful and prudent; practical turn of mind; pride and self-esteem with musical talents highly developed.

No. 11. ADELINA PATTI. Ideas are dainty, sublime, idealistic; love of admiration, display, and some ostentation; musical talents are sensuously prominent.

No. 12. VICTOR HERBERT. Constructive ability; practical ideas and aims; proud, self-reliant; an insistent nature; love of admiration is strong.

No. 13. FRANZ LISZT. Impressional and luminous mind; a perspicuous, lucid intellect; tune, harmony, and "tone" color highly developed.

No. 14. OLGA SAMAROFF. Conservation of ideas; imaginative; idealistic; quick and ready mind; apt to be boastful and ostentatious.

No. 15. THEODORE THOMAS. Good business instincts; constructive mind; highly intuitive; inspirational; musical signs are indicated.

No. 16. FRITZ KREISLER. Simple tastes and ambitions; inspirational, keen judgment; musical and artistic ambitions.

No. 17. JOSEF HOFMANN. Dexterous, clever, original, constructive; matter-of-fact nature.

No. 18. MAUD POWELL. Mistrust and subtlety of nature; vanity and love of display; desires approbation; musical powers are highly developed.

No. 19. MISCHA ELMAN. Cautious, prudent, and conservative nature; soaring ambitions with love of display and admiration indicated.

No. 20. ERNEST HUTCHESON. Highly trained mentality; imaginative, with quick perception without conscious reasoning; musically sensuous.

No. 21. EMMA EAMES STORY. Determination, firmness, will power, and courage; originality of ideas; clever, versatile, and logical.

No. 22. WALTER DAMROSCH. Self-conscious nature; originality and self-reliance; imagination; fantasy; usually impatient.

No. 23. JOSEF STRANSKY. Practical turn of mind; strong reasoning powers; instincts of a good business man; talent for music and art strong.

No. 24. VLADIMIR DE PACHMANN. Unassuming, modest, righteous; moral, clean nature; highly inspirational; a calm quiescent disposition, modified by a love of approbation and admiration. Has musical soul.

PROMINENT ACTORS, ACTRESSES, OPERA SINGERS, MUSICIANS AND COMPOSERS

1.	MARCELLA SEMBRICH	Inspirational, with love of admiration.
2.	I. J. PADEREWSKI	Love of display; mistrust and subtlety of nature.
3.	MENDELSSOHN	Protectiveness; vanity; simplicity of tastes, although a slightly intriguing personality.
4.	ENRICO CARUSO	Love of admiration; a complaisant nature.
5.	L. VON BEETHOVEN	Irrascibility; brusque but honest nature.
6.	GUGLIELMO FERRERO	Good natured; benevolent and gracious of manner.
7.	WILTON LACKAYE	Strong reasoning powers; culture; peace loving nature.
8.	LUISA TETRAZZINI	Coquetry and fun loving; loves to be admired; tenacity of purpose.
9.	MARY GARDEN	Courage with a certain sensuousness and love of finery.
10.	ELSIE JANIS	Depreciative nature; generosity strong.
11.	ELLEN TERRY	Great tenacity of purpose; physical courage and sensuousness of form and display.

PROMINENT ACTORS, ACTRESSES, OPERA SINGERS, MUSICIANS AND COMPOSERS

12. EMMA CALVE — Lover of the artistic; an aesthetic nature; faddish.

13. CLARA L. KELLOGG — An insistent nature, in which the materialistic is strongly manifested; selfish.

REPRESENTATIVE VAUDEVILLE ARTISTS

The men and women who are affiliated with the vaudeville branch of the theatrical profession represent a distinctive element among public entertainers in that they are individually expert in some particular novelty, excelling in it according to its specific character. The few specimens of signatures shown here are among the "top notchers" in their profession. Each one is representative of their special calling. The tendencies seem comparative, in that all show more or less of imagination, versatility, and earnestness, yet are lacking in the higher attainments possessed by professionals in the drama and operatic lines; they all possess the same love of admiration and approbation which are characteristic of them.

No. 1. GEORGE BEBAN. Great determination and tenacity of purpose; desire for culture and education; a certain refinement and aspiration for the idealistic.

No. 2. BLANCHE BATES. An insistent, stubborn nature; highly imaginative; strong willed; extremely affectionate.

No. 3. MARSHAL MONTGOMERY. An insistent, persistent, stubborn nature; vivacity, quickness, animation, with much hastiness; intolerant of details; great tenacity of purpose.

No. 4. EVA TANGUAY. An erratic, animated, vivacious nature; great physical alertness and restlessness; cautious; suspicious.

No. 5. IRENE FRANKLIN. Self-interest is the governing motive; self-conscious nature; seldom does things impulsively; little regard for authority.

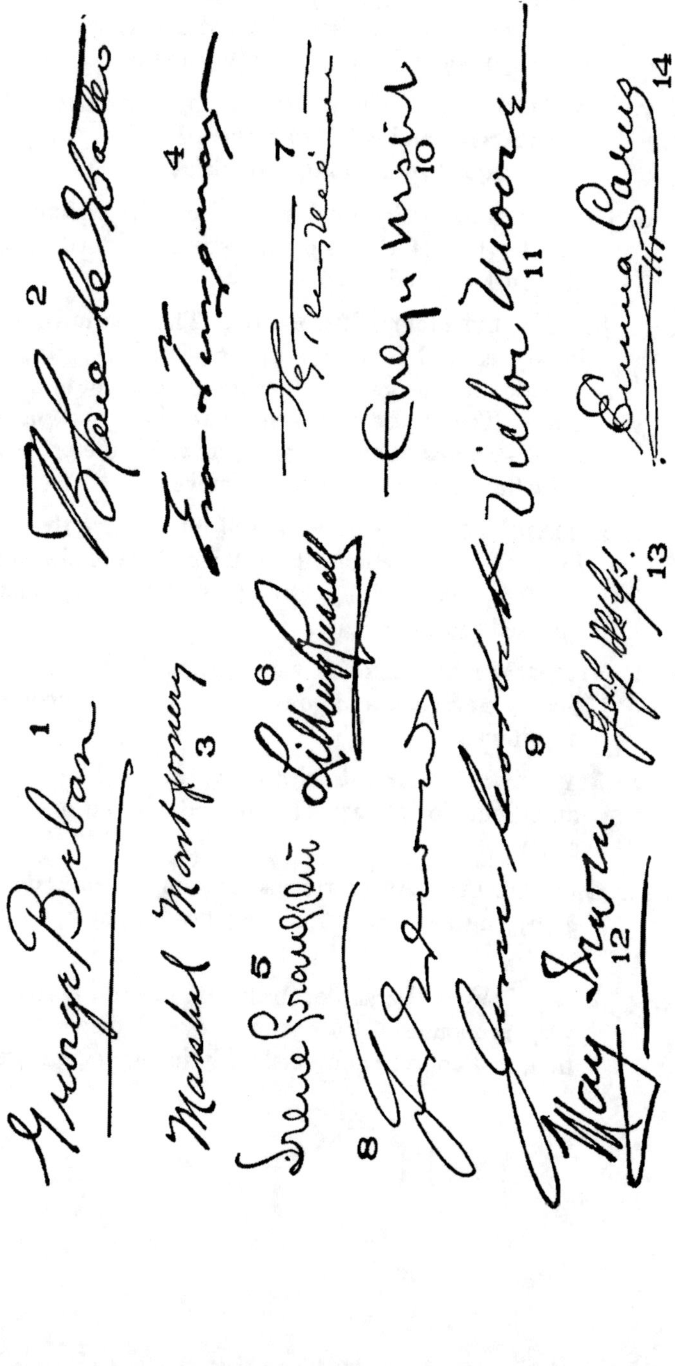

REPRESENTATIVE VAUDEVILLE ARTISTS

No. 6. LILLIAN RUSSELL. Quietly self-appreciative nature; fondness for approbation strongly indicated; vanity and a bit of egotism, with love of display and pride.

No. 7. FAY TEMPLETON. Guided largely by impressions; mild eccentricity, and slight exaggeration; a vainglorious nature; quick, observant, and critical.

No. 8. GUS EDWARDS. Practical turn of mind; argumentative and skeptical of what is not at once understood; opinionated with decided views.

No. 9. JIM CORBETT (James J. Corbett). This specimen written in so free and friendly a spirit, signifies a kindly and affectionate disposition, unostentatious and unpretentious. The object of this specimen is to show a signed name stripped of all formality, in which the professional glare has been unconsciously removed.

No. 10. EVELYN NESBIT. Reason and self-interest are the governing motives; accepts little on faith; love of pleasure and comfort, actuated by strong animalistic instincts, as opposed to the spiritual.

No. 11. VICTOR MOORE. Lacking a strong, resolute nature, modified by cleverness and powers of mimicry; immoderately ambitious.

No. 12. MAY IRWIN. Clannish with great love of kin; versatile, ambitious, jovial nature; endowed with strong common sense.

No. 13. GABY DESLYS. An avaricious, grasping nature; desire for gain; cautious and suspicious; headstrong and opinionated.

No. 14. EMMA CARUS. Versatile; brilliant; mental activity of a very pronounced description; love of display, admiration, and approbation; a slightly intriguing nature.

ABNORMALLY LARGE HANDWRITINGS

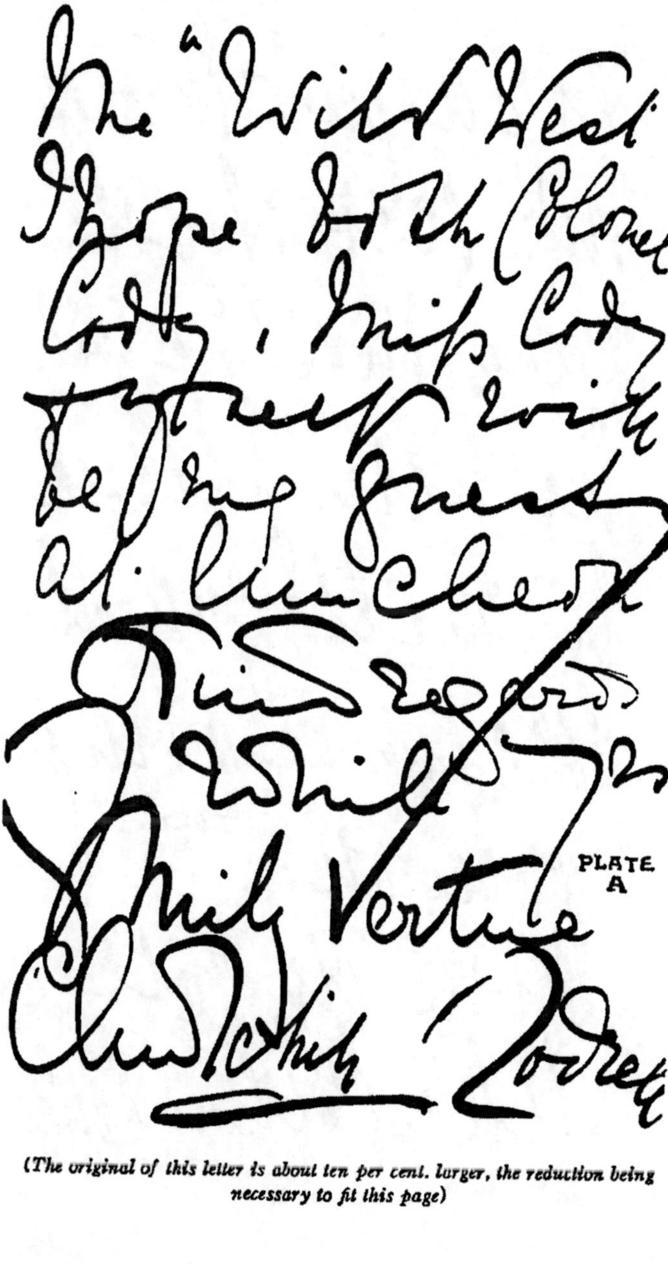

PLATE A

(The original of this letter is about ten per cent. larger, the reduction being necessary to fit this page)

ABNORMALLY LARGE HANDWRITINGS

Straight-through
Mr. Beresford
says that he will
be very pleased
to meet you at
Greenore & bring
you on.
How do you
like Birmingham

PLATE B

(Fac-simile)

ANOMALIES OF HANDWRITING

ABNORMALLY LARGE WRITING

The specimens shown on the two preceding pages indicate the synthetic rather than the analytical mind.

These specimens were written by ladies of the English nobility whose lives are pampered and petted; whose every material wish is granted, rendering them extremely sensitive concerning their favored surroundings, and jealous of their social standing.

Compared with people of normal living and habits these persons of the "upper class" must find an outlet for their effulgent ideas about entertaining and of being entertained, for they are wont to live and do things in a larger way than those living in a lower plane. This habit of being "big" is reflected in the handwriting.

This bold style of writing proclaims the individuality of the person; it says as clearly as anything can be said: "I am big; I am lofty; I am grand, august, and divinely selected to be your superior." The script suggests a natural tendency to display outwardly the person's manner of carriage, poise, and station; the expression of self; they feel a right to be big, daring, courageous, bold, proud, resolute, and critical.

When the emotions have been over stimulated the impulses become correspondingly aggressive, rendering the nerve forces active under great tension, which draw heavily on the physical resources, and threaten the vitality. This sapping of the vital fluids, sooner or later warps the intellect and weakens the mental processes, inducing prejudices that narrow down to small mental compass. The result is a "high-brow," or synthetic mind.

Generally speaking, "high-brows" or persons who aspire to look at things "above the common herd," move under great tension. This strain must find relaxation in some form of emotional outburst, which, for the want of better means, turns to entertaining their peers, or other social functions, or responding to them; in either case the mental strain is the same.

The nature develops a materiality in which the affairs of life tend to the grosser, away from the spiritual; they become notional, indulgent, effusive, and talkative. The critical and emotional senses grow acute. Because of this inherent desire for show and exploitation of self, they are apt to express their feelings without reserve.

This encompassment of surroundings renders these individuals narrow in their mental grasp of things, lacking concentration, or the power to see or feel beyond their own little world, and in consequence their thoughts, like their writing, are diffuse and fly readily from one subject to another. While morality and integrity are not necessarily less, they are certainly blunted; in most instances sensuality is an accompaniment.

Plate A is an unusual specimen of abnormally large writing, and for this reason much interest attaches to it. The veriest novice in graphology can readily conclude that the writer has very little reserve force, because the energy expended in penning the letters must have been extravagantly spent. Correlative with this useless expenditure of energy the nature is to be extravagant in all ways, in the spending of money, in the expression of opinions, charities, vocabularies, and deportment. In the vernacular of the day, she is "up in the air."

Plate B, also the writing of a woman, takes on nearly all the characteristics of the writer of specimen A, with the possible exception that she is less appreciative of her exalted position, although equally imbued with this sense of superiority. Her nature is one that is readily animated, excited, venturesome, vivacious, and spirited. She is talkative, has much to say about herself, her personal affairs, and experiences, and while an entertaining talker, her one thought is about herself and her petty recreations and social functions. Both specimens denote selfishness and thoughtlessness of an extreme depth.

An analysis of either specimen will reveal many other interesting features, which are held in reserve for the student, and from which he will derive profitable experience.

MISFITS AMONG BOOKKEEPERS

There is only one job a man loves best and can do best and from which he will profit most; that is the job for which he is best fitted by nature.

Mr. Frank A. Munsey, the eminent newspaper publisher, says: "You cannot get out of a man what God Almighty didn't put into him; you must suit the man to the job, not the job to the man."

Among all clerical vocations, bookkeeping is probably the most deceptive, because it appears to be what it is not; it attracts young men away from other fields that are more productive, more prospective, and remunerative. The hopes for an easy, dignified semi-professional job, is the magnet that attracts men whose natural aptitudes point to other directions.

The business schools throughout the country are grinding out bookkeepers by the hundreds, the great majority of whom are temperamentally unfit for this class of work. The labor market is glutted with applicants seeking positions as "accountants" when only about two per cent. are really competent. This has been tested by vocational counsellors and employment managers who reluctantly admit it to be a fact.

The author professionally examined two-hundred replies to one single advertisement from applicants for the position of bookkeeper, and was able to select only four out of the lot that showed any ability or natural aptitude for this work.

As a matter of business advantage, it is desirable for every man to take up a course in bookkeeping, but not necessarily with the expectation of following this work as a vocation. Its adoption will prove a disappointment to ninety per cent. of those who undertake it. The honorable profession of "keeping accounts" has greater responsibilities than the mere posting of items in a ledger. This is demonstrated by the introduction into business of the trained Certified Public Accountant, whose duties are to supervise the work done by bookkeepers. Had

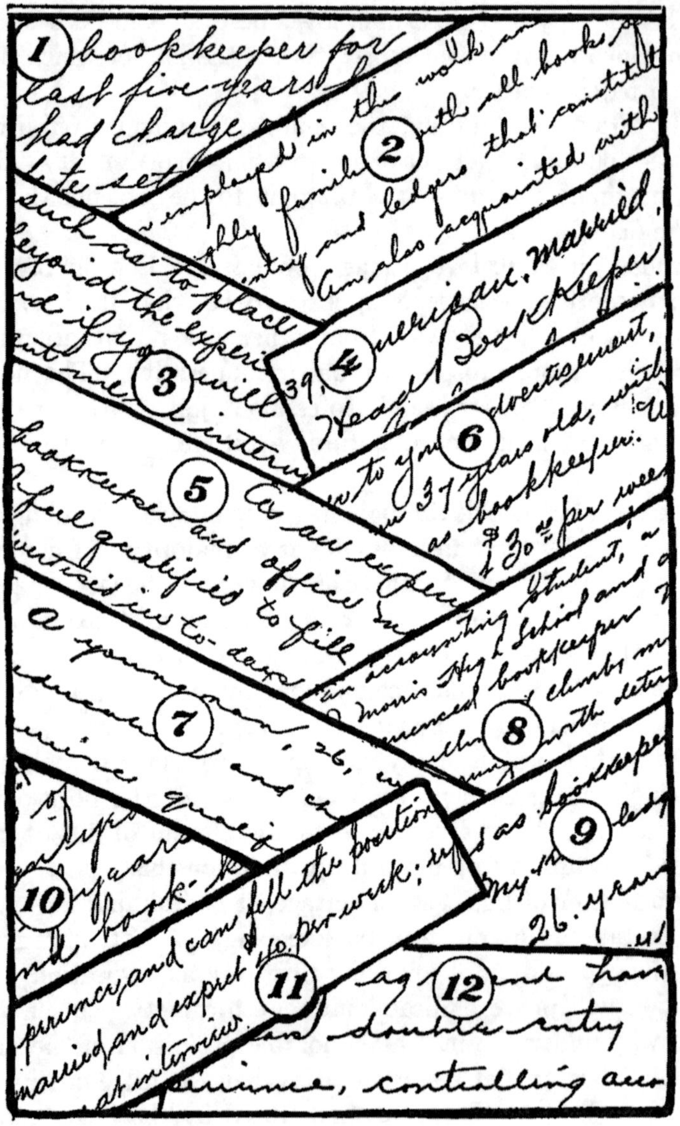

MISFITS AMONG BOOKKEEPERS

the bookkeeper been inherently adapted to the work, the professional accountant may have been unnecessary.

The specimens printed on the preceding page were indiscriminately selected from a batch of replies received from applicants through an advertisement for the position of bookkeeper. Eleven out of twelve applicants indicated would have succeeded better as farmers or carpenters than as bookkeepers.

No. 1 writes a "pretty" hand; he is insistent and sometimes obstinate; there is a dash of ingenuity. He is conscientiously honest, refined, and cultured. He is too impatient to make a capable bookkeeper, for he is unable to concentrate on details and lacks close application. This man is naturally a composer of music, or should take up theology, both of which need an inspirational temperament.

No. 2 is too wavering in mind and may be unable to thwart temptation; why not try outdoor employment, either in engineering or mining?

No. 3 is of the mental type, inert and probably indolent; lacks energy and ambition; would succeed better as a compositor, proofreader, or checking clerk.

No. 4 should have learned the trade of carpenter before he started his career as bookkeeper. He lacks mental capacity for it.

No. 5 would have made a successful correspondent, or literary man had he trained for this line of work. He has full command of language and has an active mentality.

No. 6 ought to be earning thirty dollars a day as an architect instead of seeking thirty dollars a week as a bookkeeper. This man has imagination and constructive ability.

No. 7. This young man would make a competent shipping clerk, collector, or floor walker; he is of the motive type and is out of his element in any sedentary position.

No. 8. This man is intellectually weak, lacks ambition, and has the habit of "putting off," although traces of falsehood are shown, he does not intend to deceive, but lacks the moral courage to assume the responsibility for any indiscretion. He should try chemistry.

No. 9 should seek some trade that requires limited muscular effort, for he is physically unable to do heavy work. He lacks the mental equipment for accounting.

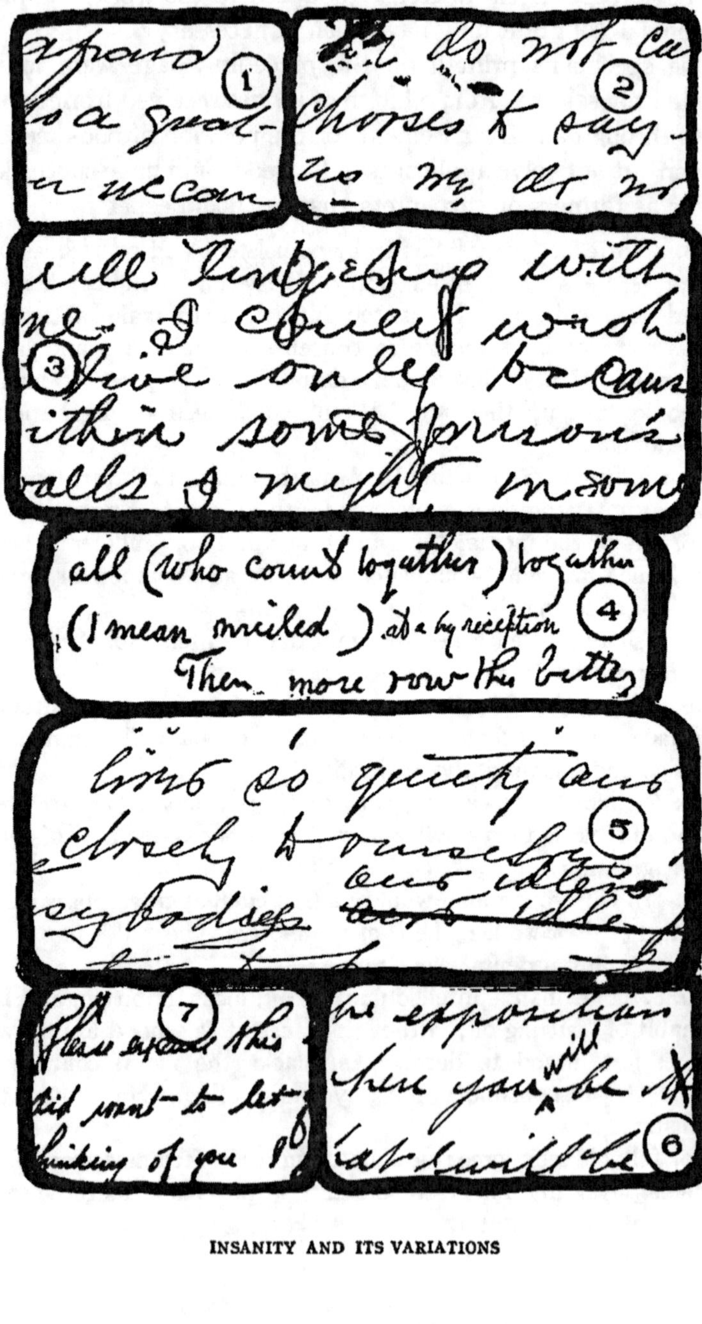

INSANITY AND ITS VARIATIONS

No. 10 will find his proper place in the ranks of road salesmen, for he is alert, strong, and broad visioned. Publicity writers are developed from material such as he.

No. 11. If this man were as persistent in seeking a job as draftsman, engraver, or letterer, he would find his proper niche. A lithographic artist or photographer's retoucher would fit him.

No. 12. Many years ago, Horace Greely attracted considerable attention of the young men of his day, by advising them "to go West" and grow up with the country. This young man has all the attributes for making an intelligent, successful farmer, and he should lose no time in embracing the opportunity. Bookkeeping and he are incompatible.

INSANITY AND ITS VARIATIONS

Insanity is divided into two general classifications, the Acute and the Chronic; these forms may be subdivided, and the subdivisions still divided, until the several varieties of insanity form a very intricate conjugation of mental disturbances.

Graphology makes no claims to supply signs for determining the different phases of mental unbalance, which are distributed over a wide range of afflictions, from the incipient, or aberrated form, to the virulent type, commonly known as crazy or maniacal. The principal forms of insanity, in their order of development, are: emotional, delusional, dementia, mania, melancholia, and paranoia.

In a collective sense writing that is exaggerated in any particular, by unusual strokes and formations of the letters, or interference of the loops of one line with the line above or below, is characteristic of mental disturbance, the form of which may be reasonably determined by the direction of the sign that controls the trait of character affected in the patient.

It is possible for insane people to write perfectly sane letters on subjects not associated with their delusions, so the subject matter may not always reveal signs of peculiarity in the patient.

No. 1. The lady who wrote this specimen would never be suspected by her friends or acquaintances of having any mental disturbance, unless her unreasonable criticisms, depressive and morbid nature, would supply any hint of the threatened indisposition. The downward cant of the writing and unsteady strokes supply the early indications.

No. 2. This specimen was written by an estimable, refined, and educated lady, a spinster of thirty-five years, who at this period of her life showed signs of mental unsteadiness, with physical outbursts of temper, quite unlike her former quiet demeanor. Specimen No. 5 in the same plate is her writing one year later, after she had been placed in an institution for the insane. Her malady was described as delusional insanity, in which she entertained hallucinations of men who were enamored of her. The nervous, excitable pen scratches, uncertain formations, frequent erasures and unconventional final "d's" with inordinate drooping of the last words on the lines, are the markings that denote her disordered mental condition.

No. 3. Is a specimen of writing of the insane, characterized as passionate, emotional excitement, with an erotic nature, and known as the form *Mania.* The diffused, yet cramped gathering of the letters, uncouth formations, and the intrusions of the loop letters on the lines above and below, the irregular base line and the divergent strokes, with a weak, characterless arrangement of the words, are the signs that describe this writer's mental twist. Notwithstanding these irresponsible pen marks, there are evidences of former refinement and culture, education and highly developed intellect, that seems to have tottered and fallen away. The inevitable course that follows uncontrollable sexual desire. This is thewriting of the young divinity student, Rev. Clarence V. B. Richeson, who murdered his fianceé, at Boston, Mass., and was executed.

No. 4. This is a specimen of the writing of a *Paranoiac.* This patient was confined in an institution, under legal restraint, after having been adjudged insane, following the shooting of a prominent man, whom he charged with violating his confidences with his wife. The writing of paranoiacs is easily distinguishable from the other forms of insanity, by examining the incoherency and confused arrangement of the words, the distorted phraseology and disordered lines and spacing; the irregular formations of the letters, the connections, omissions of words and letters, the particularization of events and things, jumbled together, showing the confused state of mind and erratic tendencies.

No. 5. This specimen has been discussed in paragraph No. 2.

No. 6. This specimen was taken from the writing of a habitual crook and thief, whose mental balance was affected. This man, while not sufficiently insane to be restrained, resorted to theft, because of an abnormal development of the bumps of covetousness and wilful disregard of the rights of others. His pen marks indicate one who may have had the benefits of education and refined surroundings, but his natural bent for bold, reckless and unreasonable avarice, displays an unbalanced mentality, which accounts for his unstable conduct. This specimen was excluded from the plate devoted to criminals, because it partook more of the irresponsible feature in crime, than because of deliberate wrongdoing.

No. 7. The writer of this specimen was not adjudged insane, but his unnatural propensities, nevertheless, put him in the class of those whose mentality has become warped and twisted. It is the alleged handwriting of "Oliver Osborne" whose alleged escapades with a young woman were responsible for the notoriety given to a prominent lawyer, whose name was associated with the scandal. The script displays the mental perverseness of the libertine, one whose habits are œstrual, demeaning, and low down in the scale of human baseness. Evidently an attempt had been made to disguise the hand, but the tell-tale marks were unconsciously permitted to remain, denoting a keen intellect, with deductive reasoning powers, great energy and ambition to succeed, broad vision and trained faculties, with hasty, animated, impulsive, and erotic impulses. The natural hand (if this is a disguise), should have been less compressed and rounded. The only excuse for placing this specimen in this plate is to show to what moral depths even the intellectual may descend.

CROOKS, THIEVES AND DEGENERATES

The grapho-psychological survey and measuring of people's values, morals, and actions, open the door to an acquaintance with many men and women who follow crime for a livelihood.

No. 1. A specimen of the script of Henry Starr, the Western highwayman, written to his young son just before he renewed his life as an outlaw. The wavy base, cramped letters, tied *s*, pointed tops, and variable size of the letters, reveal him as a keen, bold,

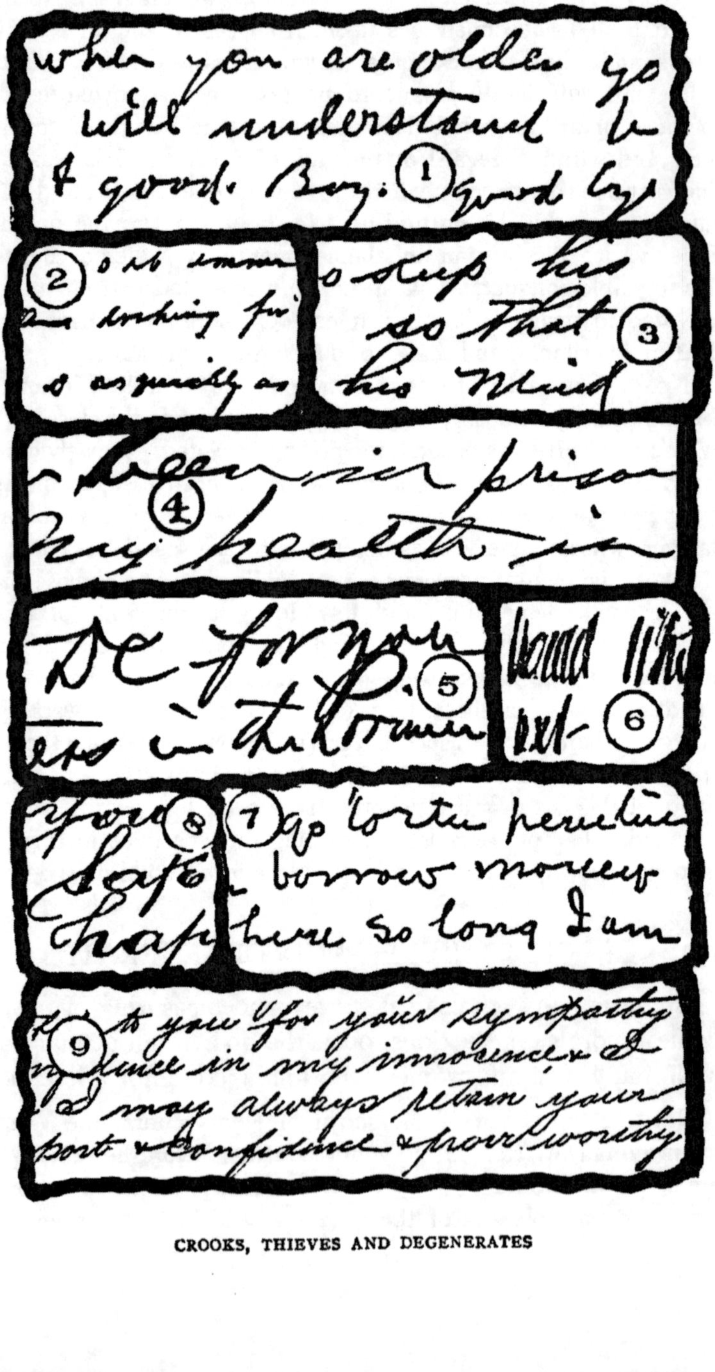

CROOKS, THIEVES AND DEGENERATES

cunning type of man; the decreasing letters and undulating finals, mark him as the relentless criminal that he is.

No. 2. The pen mark of a sentimental old reprobate; his undoing was in confiding in his stenographer, who was unable to hold a secret. Despite the writer's caution in financial matters, this confidence was innocently betrayed, and ended in his apprehension and conviction for fraud.

No. 3. The sluggish hand of a drug fiend, who, under its influence, was swayed to dishonest actions. His strong *t* crossing indicates that there remained in him a fragment of decency and honor, now lost in irresolution and fear, which grew into a fiercely vicious state of mind, and brought him at last to live as a procurer, the vilest kind of thief. The tied *s*, the *d* final below the line, the wavy base, the excessive slant of the writing—all testify to his perfidy—a degenerate in mind and body.

No. 4. The muddy, vulgar scrawl in this specimen is the handwriting of "Bluebeard," the monster who confesses to having put to death nine of his score of wives. He is J. P. Watson, now serving a life sentence at San Quentin prison, California. Note the undulating base, irregular letters, heavy and light uncertain strokes, crowded lines, and smeary, irresolute strokes, all characteristic of an unbalanced, yet pervert mind.

No. 5. Specimen from the handwriting of a public official, who was convicted of graft and misappropriation of funds. The bold heavy hand, decreasing size of letters, hooks on *t* bars and closed *o's*, stamp him as a crafty, tricky person, full of intrigue and cunning.

No. 6. These peculiar and extraordinary scratches depict an unbalanced nature, ready to take any risk in dissipation. Every down stroke spells moral and physical cowardice.

No. 7. This is a woman's script; she is by nature possessed of an active, clear mind, and bright intellect, but with an undercurrent of odd perversity, which through strain on the nervous system, developed into kleptomania, with apparently no control over her actions. The variable and wavering lines, the irregular slopings of the letters, and their variable sizes and placing on paper are the tell-tale marks. Truly this is an illuminating specimen; it determines some mental disorder as the base of her peculiarities.

No. 8. The heavy, vulgar shading, unkempt and coarse strokes, show dissipation and vicious living. Though intelligent, he is a dangerous beast, bristling all over with selfishness, a detestable and moral coward, a veritable lounge lizard, a frequenter of the bawdyhouse.

No. 9. This specimen is far above the average among criminals; it denotes culture and refinement gone wrong, rarely seen in men with brutal, fiendish instincts. This script is the boastful, pompous mark of the retroactive mind. It proclaims self-glorification. The writer of this specimen was a proud official, high in the councils of the New York Police Department. Intoxicated with powers bestowed upon him, he instigated the murder of a noted gambler, was convicted of the crime, and executed.

ILLITERATE HANDWRITING

The specimen shown on the preceding page is a missive received by a patent medicine manufacturer, which for a while baffled the office force. The interesting feature about this letter is the tutored formation of many of the characters in the writing; this suggests that the letter may have been written by some wag for the purpose of hoaxing the manufacturer. This inference might be feasible without careful examination of some of the minor parts of the strokings, which plainly reveal the untutored hand. The small letter *r* is consistently substituted by the capital letter, which is also seen in the letter *b*. Another tell-tale evidence of illiteracy is the crude manner of crossing the *t*, all of which lacks intelligence and force of mental training, indicating an ignorant person laboriously trying to write a letter. The following is a parenthetical "translation."

Santelouis (Saint Louis) Mo (Mo.) Ocotbe (October) JiRSte (First) M Riwon teto (Mr. I want to) askeuyoua Queston (ask you a question) aBoutemicas (about my case) ihaVeBwen (I have been) stRicteD (stricken) J-(f) ol 'uy e a Ran iante (for one year and ain't) weluy eat (well yet) iha V B wen Dil at (I have been die—dead-lot) Mo R thena Doznti mes (more than a dozen times) ntwellyeat (not well yet) Paragraph: GaVe (give) maiDesme (medicine) ("for" omitted) itiJ (f) uyou Please (it if you please) ANceRS oanto Rhicks (Answer soon to R. Hicks) NoRth CoMP-toN 22 (North Compton St.) iwil Pauyouwel (I will pay you well).

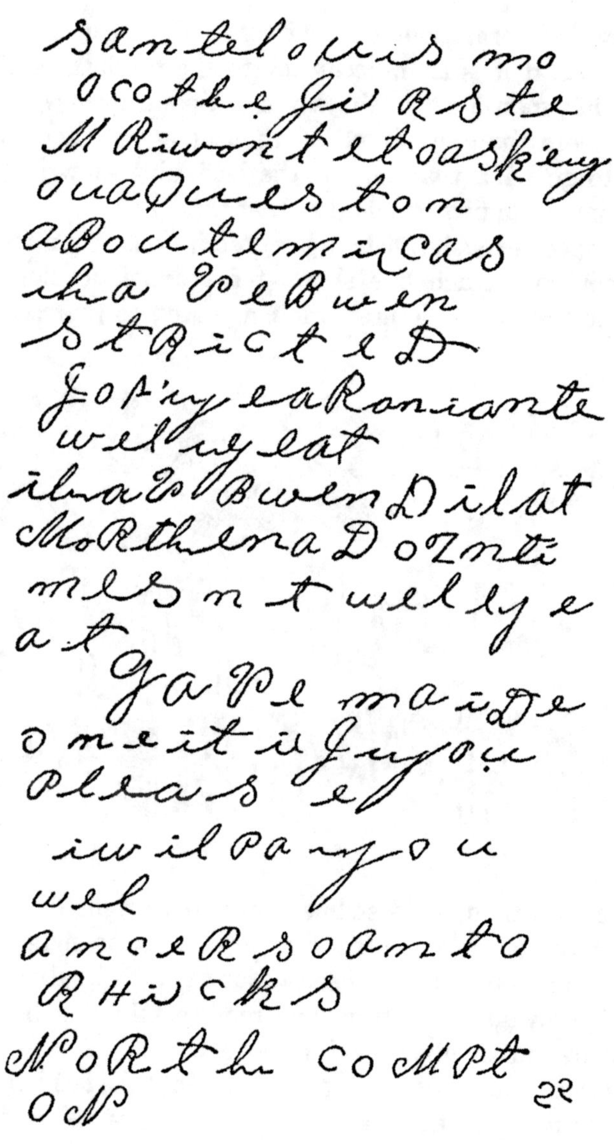
santelouis mo
ocothe Ji RSte
MRiwontetoaskey
ouaQueston
aBoutemicaS
iha VeBwen
StRicteD
JoPinyeaRoniante
welyeat
ihaVBwenDilat
MoRthenaDoZnti
meSnt wellye
at
GaVe maiDe
omeitiJuyou
PleaSe
iwilPayou
wel
anceRsoanto
RHicks
NoRth coMPt
oN
22

HOW WRITING DEVELOPED FROM PICTURES

Graphic information is so old that no one can date it with accuracy. If it is true, according to the revelations of geologists, that man lived in the caves of Spain, France, and Germany more than two hundred thousand years ago, we shall have to go back that far for the beginning of writing, as it developed from pictures used at that time.

The specimens shown here are inscriptions taken from Persian pottery. Each line shows the gradual development of crude letters from pictures originally used to represent ideas.

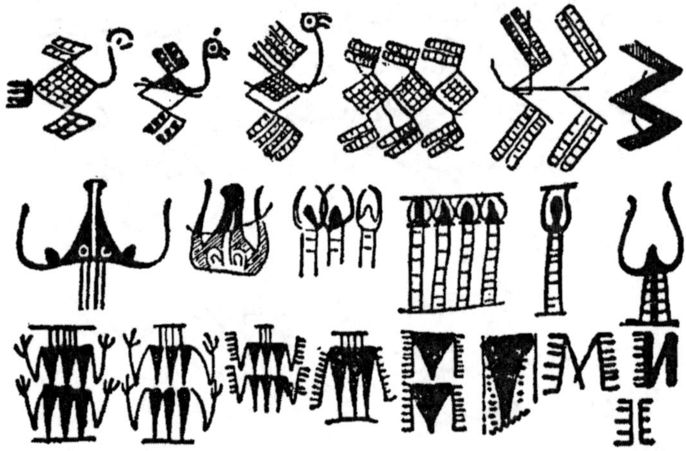

The figures on the first line from left to right show a flying bird with its development into letters. The figures on the second line represent the head of an ox, with its development. The figures on the bottom line represent human beings, terminating into symbols used for letters.

That the human mind progresses in this fashion is most clearly proved by the practices of savages and children, as well as of illiterate. All try to convey what is in their mind, either by picture writing or object-sending.

CHINESE WRITING 5,000 YEARS AGO

According to the highest authorities on Chirography, the Chinese were the first to systematize a set of characters for writing, developing an alphabet or set of symbols from the pictures that formerly served the purpose of transmitting thought. The specimen shown here depicts this development in unmistakable clearness. The right hand column are characters now used by the Chinese to express certain words in one of the Chinese dialects, while the left hand column shows the pictures they used before their alphabet was developed. The center column in script is the English translation for the Chinese words.

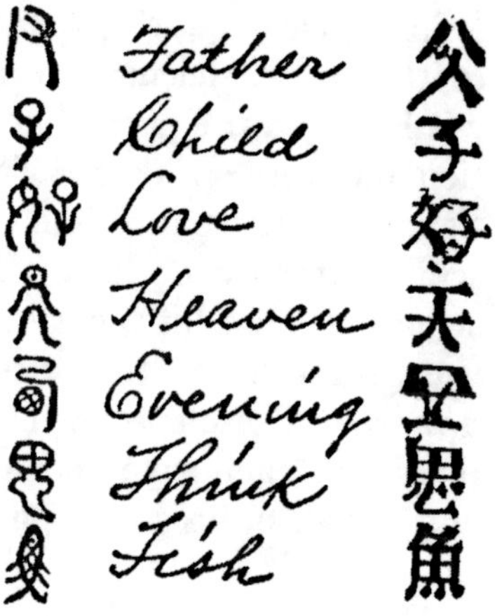

THE SIGNATURE OF "BLUEBEARD"

The confusing mass of curves and strokes that form this unintelligible signature were penned by Count Giles de Laval, Lord of Retz, who was Marshal of France in 1429. He was born in 1396, and after living a nefarious life, during which he practiced murder as a fine art, he was dubbed "Bluebeard." He was executed at the castle at Nantes, October 25, 1440.

THE SIGNATURES OF NAPOLEON

All these signatures were made on occasions calling forth widely differing emotions, and they vary as greatly as did the emotions. No. 1 is Napoleon's signature written after being crowned Emperor in 1804. No. 2 was written in Napoleon's proclamation, after his victory at Austerlitz, Dec. 2, 1805. No.

3 is the emperor's signature penned after his entrance into Moscow, Sept. 21, 1812. No. 4 shows great depression after the retreat of his army from Russia, Oct., 1812. No. 5 is his signature to a document executed at Erfurt, after the defeat at Leipzig, Oct. 23, 1813, showing great agitation. No. 6 was written at St. Helena, showing exasperation and chagrin. No. 7 is his signature penned at Fontainebleau prior to his abdication on April 4, 1814. The difference between the orderly signature written after the victory of Austerlitz and the blotted scrawl after the defeat of Leipzig is very striking. All of his signatures made at times of failure or depression have a downward slant, while that after the victory of Austerlitz slants upward. These specimens are authentic photographic reproductions, taken from documents signed by Napoleon at different periods of his sovereignty.

PICTURE WRITING UP TO DATE

These illustrations furnish a curious phase of human intelligence, being a transcript from a memorandum book kept by an illiterate woman living in one of the rural districts of Germany. Her business was to fulfill commissions in the nearby city for her country neighbors. Instead of writing her orders in the book, which she was unable to do, she drew pictures to represent the thing or things she was to purchase in the city. When she would buy rice she pictured a symbol that meant rice to her; when a customer wanted pears she drew a picture of one. The same procedure was followed to indicate a sponge, slate, for a pot and cakes, or for wine and pork.

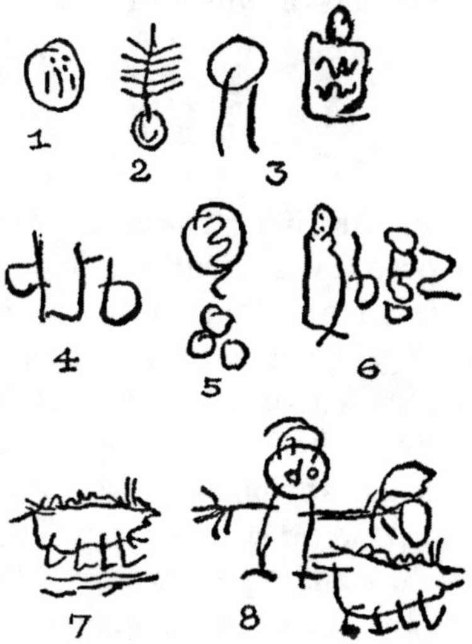

This very crude way of keeping memoranda reminds us that through just such instances as this we gain an insight into the beginning of writing, which always started with pictures, and gradually attained to symbols which developed into systematized markings; these strokes and curves, in whatever language, are formed into words and sentences, which appeal to the civilized intelligence, and are communicable to others.

The key to this picture writing is: No. 1—means rice; No. 2—is a pear; No. 3—is a sponge and slate; No. 4—is a pot; No. 5—are the cakes she is to buy; No. 6—is wine; No. 7—stands for pork (indicated by a pig) No. 8—is the bladder she is to get when the pig is killed. The memorandum book from which these pictures were taken contained several other entries similarly expressed.

EARLY BABYLONIAN SCRIPT

This is a specimen of Cuneiform writing, the first use of which dates back to a period so remote that it is idle to speculate concerning it. These markings were taken from records on clay tablets on which the early Babylonian laws were inscribed.

The Cuneiform characters of writing were wedge-shaped and believed by students of ancient hieroglyphics to have been invented by the primitive Accadians of Mesopotamia about 6,000 years ago. Some students, however, seem to doubt whether an Accadian civilization ever existed, but these signaries are believed to have been inscribed or impressed by the ancient Babylonians, Assyrians, etc., upon bronze, iron, clay, stone, and other materials. The most important of these hieroglyphics and alphabets are believed to be the Accadian, which was the oldest, its characters being idiographic. The Assyro-Babylonian was the largest and most complicated, having about 700 characters, partly alphabetic, partly syllabic, and written from left to right. The old Persian had about 60 characters, and when deciphered by Grotefend in 1802 gave a clue to other cuneiform systems.

RECORD OF AN ANALYSIS

NOTE. The convenience of this blank will be appreciated by the student, who may wish to retain a record of the specimen analyzed. Begin by filling in all spaces, with the features found in a specimen. When all the data has been collected, proceed with its delineation, according to the rules, by combining the signs, making full and frank declarations for the traits that are habitually indicated, or modify those that appear to be occasional traits.

RECORD OF AN ANALYSIS OF HANDWRITING

Name of writer.............................*Date*..............*19*....

Sex.................*Age*.............*Nature of Specimen*...........

Remarks...

....

GENERAL FEATURES

Angular or round writing............. Backhand, vertical, or forward......

Small, large, or medium writing...... Heavy, fine, or shaded writing........

Conventional or inartistic writing...... Hasty, slow, or indistinct writing....

Uniform or uneven writing........ Crowded or diffused writing............

Writing well-spaced, or not well-spaced.... Lines straight, ascend, or descend

Lines properly or improperly spaced..................................

Margins at right—wide or close to edge...............................

Margins at left—wide or narrow at top...............................

Margins at left—even or uneven......................................

Margins—both right and left wide...................................

Terminals—do they end abruptly, outwardly, upward, downward, with or without hook..

Capitals—are they plain, large, ornate, high, incurved, disproportioned, or inharmonious with body of text?...................................

Punctuation (see description)..

Capital *M* or *N*—first, second, or third strokes highest...................

Capital *M* or *N*—looped or unlooped?........ Ornamented or plain........

Capital *M* or *N*—incurved or begin with scroll...........................

Capital *M* or *N*—made with two or three vertical strokes................

Signature (see description of signs)..................................

Signature—is it confirmatory with body of text..........................

....

Base line of writing—undulating, wavy, straight, or irregular ....

Writing coarse, dirty and muddy, thick down strokes....................

SPECIAL FEATURES

Abducent or adducent writing...

Letters connected or disconnected.....................................

Lower loop letters—long, short, wide, or stroke..........................

Letters in words—do they increase, decrease; variable or uniform..........

Letters—pointed or rounded at top..................................

Initial strokes (see signs)..

Small letters *A*, *O*, *D*, *G*—are they open, closed, or looped.................

Small letter *B*—made incurve, stroke with loop, or begin with hook........

Small letter *D*, high or short stem..........looped or stroke..............

Small letter *D*—final curved up, back, to right, below line; looped or stroke..

Small letter *E*—plain or Greek form..................................

Small letter *F*—return stroke to right or left............................

Small letter *F*—made with long loops or with stroke......................

Small letter *G*—made like figure *8*, or long loop........or stroke..........

Small letter *G*—ending in triangle or return to right......................

Small letter *I*—dotted to right or left......high, over, or close to letter......

Small letter *I*—dots or dashes used........lightly or firmly made........

Small letter *I*—dot large and heavy, or circle for dot......................

Small letter *I*—dot omitted or occasionally used.........................

Small letter *M* and *N*, made like *W* and *U*..............................

Small letter *P*—lower loop long or short............or stroke..........

Small letter *P*—lower loop return on right or left of letter..................

Small letter *P*—lower point sharp and upstroke on right of stem..........

Small letter *T*—carefully, heavily, or weakly crossed....................

Small letter *T*—bar point upward or downward..........................

Small letter *T*—bar on right or left of stem..............................

Small letter *T*—bar above or down low on stem.........................

Small letter *T*—Stem begin with stroke, tiny hook, or is it looped..........

Small letter *T*—final down stroke below line or turned upward............

Small letter *T*—see list of signs for other features found in the script and note them here...

PART TWO

THE APPENDIX

FOREWORD

It is surprising how few persons can define a word correctly, off hand, without consulting a dictionary.

This appendix supplies the dual purpose of a dictionary of common phrases, terms, and words, used to denote the traits, habits, qualifications, and propensities of individuals, together with the corresponding graphological interpretations, arranged in parallel columns.

The student, in submitting his delineations of character, will frequently meet conditions where his client may want to discredit the correctness of his deductions, basing his contention on what will subsequently prove to be an incorrect knowledge of definitions, or a wrong interpretation of some word or phrase used by the student which the client may honestly believe to be adverse to what is really true.

Graphologists, and especially unprofessional students of graphology, are only human with as much knowledge of definitions as have been acquired by study and a retentive memory. The purpose of this work is to minimize errors and make the path of the graphologist as smooth as the nature of the work will permit. The principal aims sought are to avoid error and to inspire confidence in those whose incredulity must be overcome.

In writing a delineation of character the use of specific terms to give certain shades of meaning is necessary for a clear understanding of what the author intends to convey. If the interpretation is expected to carry conviction, it must be couched in simple expressive English so that the reader, the recipient, may not ascribe a totally different definition than was intended.

Any hasty, erroneous conclusion tends to discredit the work of the graphologist, although the only sins committed by the student may have been to make use of terms to express the definitions which were not properly understood by the client, and to express opinions based on belief, remote from the true definition. This temporarily causes embarrassment both to the student and the client, and may be irreparable, unless the opportunity arises for correcting the misconception of beliefs.

Most persons are apt to jump at conclusions with no regard for the standards by which proper conclusions are judged. This unfortunate trait is possessed by otherwise well-intentioned persons, but it plays havoc with results, nevertheless.

Each word selected in the appendix is carefully defined, and expressed in several shades of meaning, to conform with the part of speech in which the word is to be applied. In a parallel column is given the graphological interpretation for the trait or habit, to correspond with the analagous phrase. The significations may be verified by checking them up with the indications given in the classifications under their respective headings in either the General or Special Features of handwriting printed in the forepart of this book.

QUALIFICATIONS, TRAITS, AND HABITS

Term and Definition	*Interpretation*
ABSENTMINDEDNESS	
Lacking in attention; mind occupied with something else; habitually or frequently abstracted.	Letters omitted in words; *t*-bars above stem; *i* undotted; *t* not crossed; punctuation carelessly done.
ABSENCE OF SENSUOUSNESS	
Free from sensuousness; without this physical influence.	All cross strokes light.
ABSTRACTION	
A conception existing only in the mind and answering to no reality; something visionary; condition of mind which results in its being withdrawn from certain objects. Same as *Absentmindedness.*	Letters omitted in words; *t*-bars above stem.

Trait and definition	Handwriting signs
Accuracy (*See Precision*)	
Exactness; correctness; conforming exactly to truth or to a standard.	Punctuation carefully placed; every letter carefully made; *t*-bar neither at right nor left of stem; words frequently underscored.
Acquiescence	
Quiet submission; passive consent; compliance; disposed to yield or assent; inclined to submit.	Cross strokes absent.
Acquisitiveness	
Inclination or power to acquire; the faculty of acquiring or making one's own, by labor or effort; desire for gain.	Letters close together; hooks at end of strokes; punctuation never carelessly done; finals never long, unless used to fill blank spaces.
Acuteness	
Having a fine and penetrating discernment; keen senses; ability to make fine distinctions.	Small letters pointed at top. *m* and *n* like *w* and *u*.
Activity of Mind (*See Animation*)	
Brisk or vigorous mind.	Letters hurriedly written, some only half formed; angular hand; tendancy to small hand; well-formed letters; down strokes shaded; generally forward slope; diffused writing; well-spaced writing.
Adaptability	
Capable of adjusting one's self to situations, environments, or to changed conditions.	Uneven base line; uneven writing, not wavy base line; *m* and *n* like *w* and *u*.
Aesthetic	
Pertaining to beauty, taste or the fine arts; artistic. A person of fine taste or artistic culture. Appreciating or loving the beautiful.	Usually in the vertical, round hand; conscious writing with original formations of letters and connections; print like capitals; wide margins; wide spacing between lines; disconnected letters; capital *M* made with three perpendicular, and one horizontal, strokes.

Affection	
Desire; emotion; feeling, the giving out of the mind toward an object.	Forward slope; the more slope the more affection.
Affectation	
A studied or ostentatious pretense or attempt to display, to show off.	Flourishes; capitals too high.
Agility	
The quality of being agile; quickness and readiness in movement; nimbleness; activity of body or mind.	Angular hand; tendency to large writing; hurriedly written; not well-formed letters; writing never compressed; *p* made with lower point sharp and upstroke on right of stem; *t*-bar on right of stem or high above stem, flying off to right.
Aggressiveness	
Disposed to encroach on another's rights; to commit aggressions; to work in behalf of one's interests; to work actively; to take the initiative in an attack; to intrude.	Angular hand; heavy writing; *p* made with lower point sharp and upstroke on right of stem. *t*-bar either heavy, to right of stem, or downward.
Agreeableness (*Amiability*)	
The desire to please; suavity; blandness.	Letters extended; capitals not high; style not eccentric; down stroke of *p* rounding up to left, instead of pointed and to right; *m* and *n* like *w* and *u*.
Alimentiveness	
Desire for eating and drinking; the propensity for drinking.	All down strokes shaded; style coarse; unrefined appearance of the writing; some strokes uncertainly made.
Amativeness	
The propensity to love, or for sexual passion; faculty of love for the opposite sex; sexuality.	Right slope writing; the more slope the more passion; all down strokes shaded; muddy or unclean appearance of writing.

AMBITION

To desire and seek eagerly; an eager desire and steadfast purpose to achieve something commendable; an object of ambitious effort or purpose.

Cross strokes ascending; *t*-bars ascending; lines slanting upward, Hasty, distinct writing.

AMIABILITY (*Agreeableness*)

Kindness or sweetness of disposition; lovable.

Letters extended; *m* and *n* like *w* and *u*; capitals not too high; style not eccentric; down strokes of *p* rounding upward to left, instead of pointed and upward to the right.

AMOROUSNESS

The quality of being amorous. Having a propensity for falling in love; influenced by sexual affection or appetite; loving; ardent in affection.

Tending to flourishes in writing; fancy writing; long loops in lower loop letters; forward slope.

AMUSEMENT (*Craving for*)

A natural inherent yearning or longing for amusement.

Lines more ascending than words.

ANGER (*Quarrelsomeness, Temper*)

Animosity; exasperation; fury; impatience; indignation; passion; rage; resentment; wrath; anger is sharp, sudden, and brief.

Initial strokes absent; dashes for *i* dots; capitals never low; letters never compressed; *t*–bar higher than top of stem and at the right; *p* made with lower point sharp on upstroke at right; more likely in angular hand, tendency to vertical hand.

ANIMALISM (*Sensuality*)

Actuated by sensual instincts and appetites only; without intellectual or moral qualities; animalistic; the state or nature of an animal as opposed to higher or spiritual nature.

Down strokes muddy; writing coarse; wavy base; generally sloping hand; cross strokes heavy and dragging from one letter to another; fullness of the letters, bloated like.

Animation (*Vivacity*)

Animated; lively; quick; activity, alertness, briskness, buoyancy, cheerfulness, exhilaration, gaiety, sprightliness, vivacity.

Letters hurriedly written, some only half formed; *t* and *d* looped; letters extended; lines ascending; *t*-bar sometimes upward; either slope.

Approachableness (*Friendliness*)

Easy of access; that can be approached.

Letters extended. *m* and *n* like *w* and *u*.

Architectural Taste

Constructive; adaptation to architectural purposes; a liking for style or design of a building, a sense for building and construction.

Simple, graceful and print-like capitals; neat margins; original style of letters and joining.

Ardor

Warmth of intensity of passion or affection, or of devotion to any purpose; vehemence; zeal; enthusiasm.

Down strokes shaded; writing has upward tendency; *t*-crossings upward; well-spaced writing; generally diffused.

Argumentative

Controversial; given to arguing; disputatious; an argumentative person.

Connected letters; words occasionally connected, *t*-stem looped; *t*-bar ascending; *a* and *o* closed; tendency to heavy hand.

Arrogance

Unreasonable or excessive assumption or assertion; overbearing pride; insolence, presumption, pride, vanity, haughtiness.

Vertical writing—never sloping; capitals too high; strokes firm; intense shading—naturally done.

Artful

Characterized by craft or cunning; adroit; deceitful; designing; knowing; sharp; shrewd; tricky; wily.

Backhand writing; angularity of strokes; tendency to small hand; words close together; letters hurriedly written.

Artistic Taste	
Appealing to the aesthetic nature.	Simple and graceful capitals; wide margins—right and left; wide space between words; neat writing, never coarse.
Aspiration	
Earnest longing or earnest wish for that which is above one's present reach or attainment, especially for what is noble, pure, and spiritual; aim; ambition.	Down strokes light; cross stroke ascending; *t*-crossings upward; either slope.
Assertive	
Declarative; confident in statement; dogmatic; positive; to affirm the reality of a thing as a fact, advanced without accompanying proof.	Angularity of writing, or tops of small letters pointed; usually in large hand, or larger than medium.
Athletics	
Physical exercises.	Lower loop letters long; *p*-stem short above—long below; down stroke firm and shaded; normal, steady hand.
Austerity (*Sternness*)	
Gravity or vigor in conduct or attitude towards others; failure to show leniency; habitual, severe self-restraint or discipline; sternness.	Strokes firm, style fixed; not sloping hand; *m* and *n* unlike *w* and *u*; letters not extended; punctuation carefully done.
Autocracy (*Despotism*)	
The rule or authority of an autocrat; the autocracy of will among the faculties.	Cross strokes ascending; capitals too high; strokes growing heavier towards end; hooks at end of strokes.
Avarice	
Passion for getting and keeping riches; covetousness; miserliness.	Vertical or backhand writing, rarely forward slope; letters crowded together; final letters hardly finished; hooks at end of strokes; punctuation carefully done.

Bashfulness

State or quality of being bashful; shrinking modesty; coyness; diffidence; modesty; reserve; shyness; timidity.	Letters compressed; no flourishes; capitals low; cross strokes straight.

Benevolence

Disposition to seek the well-being or comfort of others; desire to alleviate suffering or promote happiness; love of mankind; kindliness of heart; charitableness.	Letters extended; upstroke of lower loop letters turns up to right instead of left; forward slope.

Blues

Low spirits.	Last word of line descending or drooping.

Boastfulness

To speak ostentatiously; to brag; set forth with pride or vain glory. To possess with great satisfaction.	Letters extended; *t* and *d* looped; capitals too high; large capital *I*.

Boldness

To possess audacity or fearlessness —physical or moral; daring, courageous, brave; lack of proper modesty or moderation; forward, brazen; regardless of limitations or restrictions; audacious, striking, vigorous.	Letters never compressed; finals ascending to right; *p* made with lower point sharp and upstroke on right of stem; lines straight; capitals never low; stroke firm; style fixed.

Bravery

State of being brave; valor, gallantry; heroism; having or showing courage or daring under trial; intrepid; courageous; stout-hearted.	Final and cross strokes ascending to right; strokes becoming heavier toward end; capitals too high; hooks at end of strokes.

Broadminded

Liberality of belief, opinions, and toleration.	Words well spaced on lines.

Brusqueness

Rough or rude in manner or speech; blunt; off-hand.

Small letters not smaller at end than at beginning of word; small letters *a* and *o* open; lines straight; *m* and *n* unlike *w* and *u*.

Brutality

State or quality of being brutal; coarseness, cruelty; savageness; a brutal or inhuman action.

Small letters constantly varying in size; down strokes muddy; backhand or vertical slopes; no incurve; letters never extended; capitals ungraceful; *m* and *n* unlike *w* and *u*; coarse, ungraceful style.

Buoyancy

Power of resisting or recovering from depression, discouragement, self-depreciation, or the like; elasticity of spirits.

Lines prominently ascending.

Buoyancy Restrained

To keep the spirits in subjection.

Words more ascending than lines.

Business Ability

The state or quality or training that enables one to conduct an enterprise with good judgment, thought, energy, skill, and keen foresight.

Note. For Literary, Musical and Artistic Abilities refer to headings under these titles.

Small letters neither very low nor very high; strokes and loops of one line clearly separated from lines above and below; small letters pointed at top; punctuation carefully placed; margins never wide; *t* carefully crossed; letters not widely spaced; small letters decreasing in size; signature strong and fluently written.

Candor (*Frankness*)

Freedom from mental reservation; openness; the quality of frankness or outspokenness; freedom from prejudice or mental bias; impartiality; fairness.

Small letters *a* and *o* open at top; lines straight; capital *D* open at top. Either slope—backhand excepted.

Capability	
One possessing power or capacity to do; having adequate ability; efficient; able; qualified.	Well-spaced, uniform writing.
Caprice (*Capricious*)	
A sudden change of mood, opinion, purpose, method, without adequate motive; a whim; freak; capriciousness.	Style constantly changing.
Causticity (*Sarcasm*)	
The quality or state of being caustic; figuratively, biting satire or sarcasm; satirical.	Small letters *d* and *t* sharply written with pointed stems.
Calmness	
Composure; quietness; quietude; serenity; steadiness; stillness; tranquillity; feeling without agitation; the result of strength, courage, and trust.	Round dots for periods; round hand; fine writing; even and generally well spaced writing; *t*-bars low down on stem.
Carefulness	
Exercising care; giving close or watchful attention; attentive and prudent in home, business, or duties.	Punctuation carefully placed; *t* is crossed and *i* dotted: *t*-bar never flying off to right of stem; left margins even; normal steadiness of hand.
Carelessness	
Without proper care; neglectful of danger, interest, responsibility, or duty; unconcerned; not attentive; want of care.	Punctuation carelessly done; omission of *t*-bars and *i* dots occasionally or carelessly placed.
Caution	
Considering the consequences before acting; wary; prudent; watchful; reluctant to incur danger.	Dashes used in place of, or additional to, periods; period after signature; capital *D* closed and looped at top.

Trait	Indication
Ceremoniousness	
Observant of ceremony; adherence to forms; etiquette; studiously polite; formal; having a formal character; characterized by ceremony.	Beginning stroke with flourishes.
Charity (*Charitable*)	
The spirit of charitable giving; benevolence; love and good will; kindly lenient; inclined to look on the best side.	Forward slope; the incurve; finals long and extending outward.
Changeableness	
Changeful; inconstant; likely to change or vary.	Style of writing constantly changing.
Cheerfulness	
A state of moderate joy or gaiety; good spirits; alacrity; buoyancy; animated by agreeable feelings; joyous; lively; cheery.	Lines ascending.
Clearness of Ideas	
Quick perception of mind.	Strokes and loops of one line clearly separated from lines above and below; small letters pointed at top.
Clannishness	
Having a strong feeling of fraternity; clinging or disposed to cling together. Influence by class prejudices; narrow in sympathy.	Upstrokes of lower loop letters curving well to the right.
Coarseness	
Showing lack of refinement or modesty; low; vulgar; indecent; brutish, common, ill-bred.	Style of writing is coarse and ungraceful; cross strokes are heavy; left margin uneven.
Coldheartedness	
Lacking in sensibility or emotion; unsympathetic; unfeeling; indifferent.	Backhand writing.

Combativeness	
The fighting or contending quality; quickness to engage in conflict or dispute; faculty of courage; the tendency to assail; defend; contradict and take the opposite side.	Either slope; letters never compressed; *p* made with lower point sharp and upstroke on right of stem; strokes firm; capitals never low; finals never ascending to the right.
Command of Language	
Power to obtain, use, dispose of or control language; a mastery.	Style is easy, running hand; *t* and *d* looped; either slope.
Communicativeness	
Ready or inclined to communicate; ready to impart knowledge or information; frank; talkative; ready to give, impart, or share; liberal.	Small letters *d* and *t* looped. *a* and *o* open at top.
Companionableness	
The quality or state of being companionable; capable of being, and inclined to be a pleasing companion; sociable, agreeable, friendly, amiable.	Small letters *m* and *n* like *w* and *u*; letters extended; capitals not too high; down strokes of *p* rounding to the left rather than pointed to the right. *t* bar low down on stem.
Composure	
Tranquillity of feelings, thought, manner of appearance; calmness, serenity, repose; self-control, fortitude, courtliness.	Punctuation dots round; strokes firm; *t*-bar not at right of stem; finals descending to right; down strokes concave; capitals not low and never complicated; style graceful and cultivated; *m* and *n* like *w* and *u*.
Conceit	
Vain conception of one's own person or accomplishments.	Words close together; capitals too high; first stroke of capital *E* inflated; flourishes in writing.
Concentration	
The faculty of fixing one's attention upon a single object.	Small letters very low; small writing rather than large script; capitals and small letters plain without flourishes or ornamentation.

CONCILIATION	
Overcoming enmity or hostility; act of obtaining friendship.	Strokes becoming heavier towards end with little tails added.
CONFIDENCE	
The state or feeling of trust; feeling of security; self-reliance, boldness or courage in consequence thereof; assurance carried to the extreme.	Finals or dashes *not* used to fill out otherwise blank spaces.
CONFUSION OF IDEAS	
(Not meaning insanity or dementia.)	Strokes and loops of one line entangled and running into the lines above and below; not well spaced writing; letters *t* and *i* frequently uncrossed or undotted; final letter to words sometimes left off.
CONJUGALITY	
The faculty that gives desire for matrimony.	Right slope; down strokes shaded; only one form used for each letter.
CONSCIENTIOUSNESS	
Obedient to the dictates of conscience; loyal to conscience or duty; governed by conscience.	Small letters equal size, tending to increase at end of word; more generally in large hand.
CONSERVATIVENESS	
Adherence to existing order of things; disinclined to novelty or alteration as of institution or methods; opposed to change; often opposed to progress; a conservative thinker; the faculty of conservation.	General style of writing fixed; only one form used for each letter; no original style of letters or writing; adhering to old-fashioned style of capitalization and forms.

Trait	Handwriting sign
Consistency A state of compatibility and harmony of statements.	All down strokes at same angle.
Constancy Steadiness or firmness in purpose of action; calm endurance and determination; faithfulness in service and affection; certainty; veracity; assiduity; fidelity; perseverence.	Style shows only one form used for each letter; all down strokes at same angle.
Constraint The operation of power, physical or moral, compelling or preventing action. Unnaturalness in manner resulting from distrust, diffidence, or from an attempt to repress one's feelings. Syn.—Reserve.	Letters compressed; *a* and *o* closed.
Constructiveness Productive ingenuity; mechanical ability; constructive faculty; constructive reasoning.	Original method of making connections in words; odd, unusual style of writing; capitals plain and like print.
Conventionality State of being formal rather than natural; artificial character or characteristics.	Copybook style of writing; no original style of letters; style fixed; only one form used for each letter; more appearance given to penmanship than to composition.
Coquetry Trifling in love; love, gratification of vanity.	Up stroke of small letter *d* ending with graceful curve to the right.

Courage

That quality of mind which meets danger with intrepidity, calmness, or firmness; mettle, bravery; moral courage to dare to pursue a course deemed right, which may incur contempt, disapproval, or opprobrium; physical courage depends on bodily strength or intrepidity.

Finals ascend to right; stroke firm, becoming heavier toward end; capitals too low; hook at end of stroke.

Courtliness

Courteous; elegant in manners; marked by dignified politeness.

Down strokes concave; capitals not low; never complicated or ungraceful; *i* dots round; style graceful and cultivated; *m* and *n* like *w* and *u*.

Cowardice

Giving way to fear; the state or condition of being a coward.

Strokes weak; finals descend to right; writing is "scrawly," not "snappy."

Craftiness

Skilled in deceiving others; artful; cunning.

Words running into undulating strokes; last few letters in words undecipherable; *a* and *o* closed.

Creative Power

Having the power to create; productive; constructive.

Upper loop letters long; letters disconnected; original style of letters in writing.

Credulity

Being credulous; readiness to believe without sufficient evidence; proneness to accept the marvelous; easily deceived.

Capitals wide at base; finals soar high above word; *a* and *o* open.

Criticism

The act or art of criticizing; judging by some standard; formulated opinion; harsh or unfavorable opinion or judgment; censure.

Small letters very low; pointed at top; letters connected; strokes firm; style fixed; strokes and loops of one line clearly separated from lines above and below; capital *E* angular at base.

Cruelty

Disposition to inflict injury and pain; indifferent to suffering of others; inhuman.

Vertical or backhand; never the right slope, unless in the illiterate hand; *p* made with the lower point sharp and upstroke on right of stem; letters never extended; *m* and *n* never like *w* and *u*; no incurve.

Culture

Refinement of mind, morals, or tastes; enlightenment or civilization; judgment.

General style graceful and cultured; capitals not low and never complicated; strokes and loops of one line clearly separated from lines above and below. The Greek *e* and *d*.

Cunning

Crafty; shrewd; artful; tricky.

Small letters constantly varying in size; *a* and *o* closed tight; lines irregular; small letters pointed at top; finals never ascending to right; words running into undulating strokes; last few letters in words almost undecipherable.

Curiosity

Eager concern to get knowledge of or a wish to engage the mind with anything novel, odd, strange, or mysterious; often in a bad sense—a prying disposition; the quality of being curious; delicateness; nicety.

Small letters pointed at base. Finals soar upward above word.

Daring	
Possessing or exhibiting resolute courage; bold; brave; adventurous; reckless intrepidity.	Lines ascending to right; tendency to heavy writing.
Deceitfulness	
Deception; fraud; falsity; trickiness; to attempt or beguile; inclination or tendency to deceive.	Small letters constantly varying in size; lines irregular; *a* and *o* closed; *t*-stem open at base.
Decision	
The act or product of determining whether mentally or in fact; being positive and firm in one's practical judgments or actions; disposition is to prompt and steadfast action; quickness and vigor of resolution.	Down strokes firm; *t*-bar never at left of stem.
Deduction	
The power, act, or process of deducing or inferring; that form of reasoning by which a fact, truth, or statement is inferred from a general fact, law, or principle, given as a starting point; syllogistic reasoning.	Letters in words connected; *a* and *o* tightly closed; more likely in small, vertical, or backhand writing.
Defensiveness	
An attitude or condition of defense; ready for defense; to act or stand on the defensive; means of defense; safeguard.	Finals curl under to left.
Defiance	
The act of defying; to meet in combat or contest; to demand of a person proof of an assertion or accusation; contemptuous opposition or disregard openly expressed in words or action; combativeness.	Either slope; letters never compressed; *p* made with lower point sharp and upstroke on right of stem; strokes firm; capitals never low; finals never ascending to right.

Deficient Musical Taste

Not having an adequate liking or sense for music, lacking natural musical harmony; no ear for music.

Small letters angular at bottom of their last down strokes.

Deliberation

The act of weighing in the mind the reasons for and against a proposed measure or course of action; slowness and care in decision or action.

Every letter carefully made; down strokes firm; *t*-bar at left of stem or carefully crossing stem; *a* and *o* closed.

Delicacy

The quality of being delicate; fineness; daintiness; that which pleases a fine taste; fineness and sensitiveness in perception, expression, and action; a refined appreciation of propriety.

Style graceful and cultivated; all attempts at flourishing rigidly excluded.

Demonstrativeness

Able to prove beyond doubt; perfectly convincing; conclusive; inclined to strong expression of feelings or thoughts; power of clear, correct, and forcible expression.

Upper strokes long; *a* and *o* open; *t* and *d* with wide loops; letters never compressed; letters hurriedly written; some only half formed.

Depression

The state of being depressed; a falling of the spirits; low spirits, dejection; lowering of vital powers; melancholy.

Descending lines; the more the lines descend, the greater is the sign accentuated.

Designing

Taste for; sense of form.

Capitals made simple, graceful, and print-like.

Desire for Approbation

Desire for praise.

Signature flourished and underscored by some form of complicated flourish.

DESIRE FOR IMPROVEMENT

Care; a feeling of wanting to make right; desire for perfection.

Letters touched up or mended.

DESIRE FOR PLEASURE

Lines more ascending than words.

DESPONDENCY

The loss of hope and courage accompanied by mental depression; dejection of spirits, caused by ill-health, misfortune, or disappointment.

Lines very descending; the more the lines descend, the greater the sign.

DESPOTISM

Absolute power; authority unlimited; control over others.

Cross strokes ascending; capitals too high; strokes growing heavier toward end; hooks at end of strokes.

DESTRUCTIVENESS

The faculty that gives the tendency to destroy; figuratively, disregard of, or assault upon, established opinions, beliefs, institutions; iconoclasm.

Capitals too high; backhand slope; down strokes firm, tending to be muddy; in the illiterate hand, vertical or forward slopes.

DETAIL

The faculty that enables one to go into a subject minutely and with particularization.

Small writing; small letters low; *i* dots and *t*-bars carefully placed.

DETERMINATION

A firm resolve; the quality of being earnest and decided; resoluteness; firmness; the formation of a fixed purpose.

Strokes becoming heavier toward end; *t*-bars long and heavy lower loop letters ending in strokes instead of loops.

DEVIOUSNESS

Out of the path of rectitude; straying from the way of duty.

Irregular lines; *a* and *o* closed.

Devotion	
Zealous application to any pursuit or practice; strong attachment expressing itself in earnest service; ardor; zeal.	Writing very sloping; disconnected letters.
Diffidence	
Want of confidence in one's self; lack of trust in one's own wisdom, judgment or ability; timidity; self-distrust; shyness; modesty; distrust of others; lack of confidence.	Letters compressed; no flourishes; capitals low, cross strokes straight.
Dignity	
Grave or noble bearing; impressiveness of character or manner; repose and serenity of demeanor.	Down strokes concave; small letter *d* with high stem.
Dignity (Want of)	
Lack of repose and serenity of manner.	Down strokes convex; small letter *d* with low stem.
Diplomacy	
Shrewdness or skill in conducting any kind of negotiations or social matters; finesse; tact.	First letter of word larger than the rest; letters in words decreasing in size; small writing; *a* and *o* closed; plain capitals.
Directness	
The quality of being direct, and straightforward; direct and open conduct.	Straight base lines.
Discouragement	
The state of being discouraged; lack of spirit; loss of confidence.	Descending lines.

Discretion

Ability and tendency to act with prudence; instinctive perception of what is wise and proper, united with caution; the habit of wise judgment; sagacity.

First letter of words larger than the rest: *a* and *o* closed.

Dishonesty

Faithlessness; a disposition to be false, unjust, untruthful in one's character or actions; any deviation from probity or integrity.

Irregular lines; small letters constantly varying in size; *a* and *o* tightly closed; base of letters *a, o, d, g*, open; wavy base line.

Disorder

Lack of arrangement or system; without method; disregard or neglect of orderliness, rule, or conventionality in general.

Many letters illegible; left margins uneven.

Display (Love of)

Ostentatiousness.

Flourishes in writing.

Dissimulation

The act or practice of feigning; false show or pretense; deceit.

Irregular lines; small letters constantly varying in size; *a, o*, closed; last letters of words undecipherable, dwindling into mere strokes. Hasty writing.

Distrust

Disposition to withhold confidence, reliance, or faith; lack of confidence in the power, wisdom, or good intent of others, or in the safety or sufficiency of any thing or action; doubt; suspicion.

Finals long only to fill otherwise blank spaces.

Docility

The quality of being docile; amenable to training· easy to manage; tractable.

Words not connected; cross strokes never point downward; capitals never too high; words well spaced.

DOMINEER	
To exercise authority in an arbitrary way; rule with insolence or unnecessary annoyance; to be overbearing.	Unconscious shading; heavy down strokes.
DULLNESS OF PERCEPTION	
State or quality of mind that does not perceive quickly.	Small letters rounded at top.
ECCENTRICITY	
Oddity; peculiarity; idiocyncrasy, either of taste, disposition, or action.	Eccentric style of letters and writing; second or third stroke of capital *M* higher than first two strokes.
ECONOMY	
Disposition to save or spare; carefulness in outlay; frugality; economy in words or in dress; freedom from extravagance or waste.	Letters written close together; no left margin, writing is close up to edge of page.
EFFUSIVENESS	
Demonstrativeness; overflowing with sentiment; gushing.	Letters *a*, *o*, open; *t* and *d* with wide loops; letters never compressed; letters hurriedly written; some only half formed; upper loop letters long.
EGOTISM	
Conceit; egoism; self-assertion; self-conceit; self-confidence; self-consciousness; self-esteem; vanity; self-exaltation; the habit or practice of thinking much of one's self.	Capitals too high for body of writing; tendency to ornamental writing, flourishing, and effort to elaborate on the capital letters.
ELEGANCE OF MIND	
Refinement; gracefulness; polish; elegance of proportion, motion, style or manner.	Graceful and cultivated style of writing.

Elevation of Thought

Aspiration; state or condition of being elevated; exaltation; as of the mind or of material things; elevation of thought, of style, of feeling.

Down strokes lightly made; *t*-crossings ascending.

Emotions

Unusual or disturbed movement of the feelings; feelings aroused by pleasure or pain, activity or repose; may be regarded as simple or passionate emotions.

Strokes becoming lighter toward end.

Energy

Haste; zeal; activity of mind; vivacity; force; potency; vigor; habitual tendency for effective action; intensity and forcefulness in spirit and conduct; capacity for performing mechanical work.

Speed of writing energetic; letters hurriedly written, some only half formed; *t*-cross at right of stem; *t* and *d* looped; letters extended; angular hand or, if in round hand, *m* and *n* like *w* and *u*.

English Trait

This trait is chiefly found among Anglo-Saxons lacking literary training.

Finals of abbreviations, such as *r* in Mr., Mrs., Dr., etc., raised above base line; *t*-crossing looped low down on stem.

Ennui

Mental weariness produced by satietyor lack of interest; a feeling of listless tiredness; disgust or weariness; tedium.

Lines more descending than the words in the line.

Enthusiasm

Ardor; earnestness; ecstacy; fervency; inspiration; intense and rapturous feeling, felt or displayed.

Upper strokes long; down strokes shaded; cross strokes never descending.

Erratic

A peculiar or eccentric person; not conforming to rules or standards, or to what is considered proper; irregular conduct.

Uneven writing; variable size of letters; irregular spacing of lines; diffused writing.

Erotomania

Mental derangement caused by love for opposite sex; love sickness; exaggerated or uncontrollable sexual desire.

Right slope; muddy, hasty appearance of writing; *t*-bars to right or flying off stem; down strokes partially shaded; cross strokes heavy.

Exacting Disposition

Making unreasonable or burdensome demands; severe in requirements; oppressive; compelling; strict application.

Heavy writing; large or medium hand; down strokes shaded; *t*-bar dashed across the stem, some downward.

Exactness

Precision; perfectly conforming to a standard; strictly accurate or correct; to conceive or express accurately or precisely; exercising strict care or attention; methodical.

Punctuation carefully placed; every letter carefully made; *t*-bar carefully crossing the stem.

Exaggeration

Extravagantly or untruthfully presented; overstatement.

Long loops and strokes that extend to line below; excessively long loops.

Exaltation

Exuberance; a morbid mental state distinguished by ecstatic joy; abnormal optimism or delusions of grandeur; exalted sentiments.

Lines very ascending.

Excitability

Liveliness; the quality of being excitable; susceptibility to excitement.

Dashes used for periods that are much elongated and quickly made.

EXCLUSIVENESS	
Reserve, of a nature or tendency that disposes one to limit social relations.	Letters compressed; *a*, *o*, closed.
EXECUTIVE ABILITY (See *Business Ability*)	
EXTRAVAGANCE	
Excess; undue expenditure of money; profuse lavishness; prodigality; lack of moderation; extravagance of language, dress, outlay, ambition, or passion.	Diffused hand; letters and words widely spaced; margins wide; usually in large writing.
EXUBERANCE (See *Exaltation*)	
Exaltation.	Lines very ascending.
FAITHFULNESS	
Constancy; fidelity; loyalty; the quality of being faithful, true, trustworthy in the performance of duty.	Only one form used for each letter.
FANCY	
Imagination; to suppose or believe without substantial grounds; imagination.	Upper strokes long; *t*-bar above stem, to right; bar sometimes long, other times short, now and then a mere dot.
FASTIDIOUSNESS	
Fussiness; hard to please; easily repelled or disgusted; over-nice; squeamish; finical.	Small letters very low; punctuation very carefully placed.
FATALISM	
A disposition to accept every event or condition as preordained or controlled by destiny.	Final strokes to words descending vertically.

Fear

Timidity; to regard with dread, fright, or terror; to be apprehensive or afraid; desire to avoid displeasing; to doubt; to be anxious about; to suspect.

Final strokes descending to right; strokes not weak.

Feebleness

Illness; lacking muscular power; weak from disease or age; debilitated; frail; decrepit; infirm; weakly; sickly.

General style unsteady; tendency of lines to descend; upstrokes weak and unsteady.

Feeling

Sensitiveness; the capacity to feel deeply; refined sensibility shown in tenderness or ready sympathy.

The incurve (an initial stroke carried to the left of the letter before beginning the letter itself); usually seen in the capitals *M*, *N*, *U*, *C*, *E*, *K*, and in some of the small letters.

Ferocity (See *Brutality*)

Fickleness

Inconstancy; the state of being unduly changeable in feeling, judgment, or purpose; worrying; inconstant; capricious.

Frequent changes in the form of several letters.

Finesse

Subtle contrivance used to gain a point; artifice; stratagem.

Small letters smaller at end of words than at beginning; hasty writing.

Firmness

Firm will; the quality or state of being firm; solidity; steadiness; resoluteness; constancy; courage; the faculty that gives stability, persistency, and obstinacy.

Down strokes firm; *y* and *g* ending with stroke and occasionally ending with tiny hook.

FLATTERY	
Trying to influence another by the use of false or excessive praise; insincere complimentary language or conduct.	Small letters *d* and *t* with very round loops.
FLIGHTINESS	
The state or quality of being flighty; of a capricious or giddy nature or tendency; given to light-headed fancies or caprices; volatile in speech or conduct; slightly delirious.	Uneven, straggling hand; variable size of letters; *a* and *o* open.
FLIRTATIOUSNESS	
Coquetry; to act with giddy or trivial lightness; jeering or scoffing.	Forward slope; small letter *d* made with final upstroke turned gracefully to right; cross strokes scroll shape; strokes generally weak.
FLUENCY OF SPEECH	
Command of language; the quality of being fluent; ease of speech or expression.	Easy running hand; *d* and *t* looped.
FLUENCY OF THOUGHT	
Speaking or writing with facility. (Practically the same quality as *Fluency of Speech,* except that ideas or words flow more readily.)	Easy running hand; small writing; usually in the vertical; plain capitals not high.
FORGETFULNESS	
A complete ceasing to remember; being apt to forget; negligent omission; inattention.	*i* and *j* seldom dotted; *t* uncrossed; letters left out of words; punctuation carelessly done or omitted.
FORM (Sense of)	
The nature of a thing as perceived by the senses or the intellect; the instinctive ability to distinguish kind, state, or variation; the mental image or subjective view of an object highly developed.	Capitals simple, graceful, and print-like; cross strokes shaded.

Fortitude

Strength or firmness of mind to endure pain or adversity patiently; patient and constant courage; enduring courage.

All down strokes firm with finals ascending to right; *i* dots round.

Frankness

Candor; quality of being frank; ingenuousness; to be outspoken; without concealment.

Small letters *a* and *o* open.

Friendliness

Good will; the state or quality of being friendly; accessible, affable, amicable, cordial, sociable.

Letters extended; *m* and *n* like *w* and *u*.

Frivolity

Levity; a trifling act, thought, saying, or practice; frivolousness.

Crossing of letter *t* scroll shape.

Fun (Love of)

To indulge in fun; make sport; jest; the state or quality of being gay; doings prompted by spirit of light-heartedness.

t-crossing scroll shape with lines ascending.

Fussiness

Fastidiousness; making much ado about small matters; fidgety; fretful disposition.

Small letters very low; punctuation very carefully placed.

Gaiety

State of being gay; inspired by spirit of merriment or light-heartedness; fun.

t-crossing, scroll shaped.

Garrulity

Constant, trivial talking; habitually talkative; chattering; to talk overmuch.

Upper strokes very long; *t* and *d* with wide, inflated loops; *a*, and *o*, open; *b* with initial "tick" at beginning of stroke.

Generalization	
A general inference; an induction; notion, rule; thinking in terms of the concept or schematized idea.	Small letters high.
Generosity	
The quality of being generous; liberality, as of sentiment or conduct; a disposition to give liberally or bestow favors heartily; the act of giving freely and kindly.	Finals long, but not necessarily to fill otherwise blank spaces.
Generosity of Affection	
	Upstrokes of lower loop letters turn up to right instead of left.
Geniality	
Amiability; the quality or state of being genial; kindliness of disposition.	*m* and *n* like *w* and *u;* letters extended; capitals not too high; style not eccentric; down strokes of *p* rounding up to the left, rather than pointed to the right.
Gentility	
The quality of being genteel or well-bred; refinement of manners.	Style graceful and cultivated.
Gentleness	
Softness and sweetness of disposition; mildness; docility; absence of roughness.	*t*-cross close down on stem; punctuation carefully placed; round hand; vertical or right slope; fine writing; slow, easy style.
Gluttony	
The act or habit of eating to excess; gourmandizing; one who indulges in anything to excess.	All down strokes muddy; usually in large hand; either slope; coarse writing.
Gossip	
Prate, tattle, chat, idle or familiar talk.	*d* and *t* with wide loops; *a* and *o* open; strokes weak; right slope.

Graciousness

Courtliness; kindly condescension; affability; courteous bearing; mercifulness; graceful or attractive quality.

Down strokes concave; capitals not low; never complicated or ungraceful; dots round; style graceful and cultured; *m* and *n* like *w* and *u*.

Grandeur

The combination of exalted qualities in a person, that impresses the mind with a sense of imposing dignity or greatness; nobility.

Small letters high; down strokes concave; words well spaced; every letter carefully made; capitals never low; lines straight; small letters equal size; style never coarse.

Grief

Sadness; sorrow or mental distress.

Lines descending; sub-normal steadiness.

Guardedness

To exhibit caution; to be careful or circumspect in one's remarks.

Dashes in place of periods; period after signature.

Haste

Celerity of movement; unseemly quickness of action; unnecessary celerity; hurry.

Hasty writing; some letters only half formed; *t*-cross at right of stem.

Haughtiness

The quality of being haughty; expressing in speech or manner a high opinion of self and contempt for others; proud and disdainful; arrogant. Syn.—Austere; cold; contemptuous; distant; insolent; surly; unapproachable.

Capitals too high; down strokes concave.

Health

Freedom from sickness; bodily soundness; good physical condition.

Normal steadiness; lower loop letters long; down strokes shaded; strokes firm; *p* short above, long below.

HEART AND HEAD (Struggle between)	
	Loop letters at different angles.
HEART TROUBLE	
Any morbid condition of the heart whether organic or sympathetic.	Strokes notched at top of letters.
HEEDLESSNESS	
Giving no heed; careless; thoughtless.	Punctuation carelessly done.
HESITATION	
The act of hesitating; suspension of opinion; uncertainty; slowness of speech with pauses between words, arising from awkwardness, timidity, or indecision; a faltering of mind or speech.	Strokes weak; *t*-cross at left of stem; variable size of letters; one or more letters in a word written distant from the previous or succeeding letters.
HONESTY (Uprightness)	
To act justly and honorably; truthfulness; fair and candid in dealings.	Small letters equal size; lines straight; vertical or forward slope; *a* and *o* open; *d* high; last letter in word larger than first.
HOPEFULNESS	
Having qualities that excite hope; promising success; desiring with confident expectation.	Lines ascending; finals not used to fill otherwise blank spaces; *t*-cross upward.
HUMILITY	
Humble; a modest sense of one's own merit; state of mind without arrogance.	Round hand; capitals low.
HUMOR	
A facetious turn of thought; playful fancy; fun.	Finals turned up; easy running hand; letters extended; *t* bar scroll shaped.

Hypocrisy

Simulation or feigning to be what one is not; acting a false part; a deceitful show of good character, or counterfeiting a virtue; extreme insincerity; dissimulation.

Letters broken at base; last few letters in a word undecipherable; hasty, indistinct writing.

Iconoclast

Disregard of, or assault upon, established opinions, beliefs, or institutions; one who assails traditional beliefs.

Capitals too high; down strokes firm and muddy; uneven writing, generally in backhand script.

Ideality

The condition of being ideal, unreal, or imaginary; the power or tendency to form ideals.

Upper strokes long; letters disconnected; original style of letters or words.

Ignorance

State of being ignorant; lack of knowledge in general; want of information on topics embraced in the common knowledge of the world.

Coarse and ungraceful writing; punctuation incorrect or absent; spelling imperfect; slow writing, usually in large hand.

Illness

The state of being sick or ill; bodily indisposition; disease.

Sub-normal steadiness; lines descending.

Imagination

The act or power of combining the products of past experience into modified, new, or ideal forms; the constructive or creative faculty.

Upper strokes long; *t*-bar above stem.

Imitation

Faculty of imitating, that gives the abilitv to copy and conform.

Cross strokes pointing upward.

IMMORALITY	
The quality or condition of being immoral; vice; wickedness; lack of purity; licentiousness.	Tendency to heavy, coarsely-shaded writing; muddy appearance of writing; either slope; large writing or heavy small script.
IMPATIENCE	
Lack of patience; restless eagerness for change or for the accomplishment of things; intolerance of opposition or control.	Hasty writing; *t*-bar dashed off to the right; letters begin with straight, inflexible stroke; finals downward, sometimes ending with tiny hook.
IMPENETRABILITY	
The quality of being impenetrable in any sense.	Signature inclosed by sweeping stroke.
IMPETUOUSNESS	
Spontaneous or inherent energy, passion, or feeling; rushing with force or vehemence. Syn.—Excitable, fiery, hasty, headlong, impulsive, passionate, rash, swift, quick.	*t*-bar always at right of stem.
IMPORTANCE	
Weight or consequence in the social scale, in public estimation, or in self-esteem; pretentiousness.	Signature larger and different than body of writing.
IMPRACTICALITY	
The state of being impractical.	Margins wide.
IMPRESSIONABLENESS	
Subject to or susceptible of impression; easily impressed; emotional.	Writing very sloping to right; disconnected letters.
IMPROVIDENCE	
The state or quality of being improvident; lack of foresight or thrift.	Margins wide; letters widely spaced; punctuation carelessly done.

Trait	Indication
Impulsiveness The state of one actuated or liable to be actuated by impulse rather than by reason; unpremeditated.	*t*-bar at right of stem; forward slope; disconnected letters.
Inactivity (Physical) State or quality of being inactive; idleness; passiveness; sluggishness; lacking especial exertion or effort.	Lower loop letters short; round hand; *t* weakly crossed; *t*-bar weak.
Inattention Lack of attention; neglect or failure to concentrate the mind upon or give heed to something.	Letters omitted in words; small letters *i* and *j* undotted; *t* uncrossed; uneven writing; left margins uneven.
Inconsistency Not consistent; logical incompatibility; contradiction or contrariety; inconsistent in an opinion, idea, act, or the like.	Down strokes in same word at different angles; variable size of letters.
Inconstancy Instability of affection or temper; fickleness; not uniform.	Several letters made in different forms throughout the writing.
Incredulity Incredulous; a withholding or refusal of belief; indisposition to believe; skepticism.	Capitals narrow at base.
Incuriosity Lacking curiosity; uninterested; indifferent; devoid of curious or interesting qualities.	Small letters rounded at base.
Indecision Want of settled purpose or resolution; failure or inability to form a judgment, or decide on a course of action; indetermination; irresolution.	Strokes weak; *t*-bar at left of stem; varying size of letters.

INDEPENDENCE

Free from dependence upon others for guidance; self-direction or self-support; a spirit of self-reliance.	Strokes firm; original style of letters or words; lines straight; capitals not low; finals never descending to right.

INDIFFERENCE

Unconcerned, indifferent, apathetic; lack of interest or feeling regarding what is presented to the mind.	Cross strokes descending.

INDIFFERENCE TO LUXURY

	Lines close together; not well-spaced writing.

INDIVIDUALITY

Individual or distinctive character; personality; the connected development of the activities characteristic of a person.	Original style of letters or form of words.

INDOLENCE

Indisposition to exertion, arising from love of ease; habitual idleness; laziness.	Writing slowly drawn; large, round hand; *t* uncrossed or those that are crossed made with curved bar, with ends turned downward.

INDUSTRY

Habit of attention; devotion to any useful or productive pursuit, work, or task, manual or mental; earnest, steady, or constant application to business.	Angular, small hand; vertical, medium hand, with pointed tops; energetic writing; *t*-bar either carefully placed or at right of stem or across stem.

INFIDELITY

Lack of fidelity; unfaithful to a trust, duty, or vow; untrustworthiness.	Letters broken at base; coarse, muddy down strokes; closed *a* and *o*; looped *o*.

Ingenuity

The quality of inventive power; cleverness in contriving, combining, or originating; aptness; skill; intellectual ability; talent.

Original method of making connections of letters and words; odd or unusual style of writing.

Ingenuousness

Candid; frank or open in character or quality; free from reserve, disguise, equivocation, or dissimulation.

Small letters larger at end than at beginning of word; *a* and *o* open.

Initiative

The power to originate or start; the aptitude to develop or undertake new enterprises; the power of initiating.

Usually in vertical hand; well-formed letters; uneven writing; letters disconnected; natural shading; lower loop letters ending in stroke and tiny hook; joining two letters by an original cross stroke: *t* heavily or carefully crossed—some upward.

Inquisitiveness

Addicted to investigation or research; inclined to the pursuit of knowledge; given to questioning; prying into; curiosity.

Letters with oblique angles at base; Greek *e;* sharp base line.

Insanity (See *Unbalanced*)

The principal forms of insanity are: delusional, dementia, mania, melancholia, and paranoia. Graphologically defined, insanity is a deranged mental condition such as deprives a person of the capacity to comprehend the nature and consequences of a particular act; morbid condition of the mind.

Diffused writing; letters illy formed; uneven writing—straggling over the line; lines crowding each other; lower loop letters extending into lines below; not well-spaced lines; small letters constantly changing and varying in size; *t*-crossings weak.

Note. The writing of an insane person may vary from the above, according to the form of morbidity.

Insight

Power or faculty of acute perception or understanding; intellectual discernment; penetration; intuition—whether that power is regarded as a general inner faculty, a special capacity for, or the gift of, mystical vision.	Small letters pointed at top; disconnected letters; fine writing; high capitals.

Insincerity

Lack of sincerity; duplicity; dissimulation; deceitfulness.	Backhand writing; decreasing size of letters; hasty writing.

Insistence

The act of insisting; urgency; to be persistent.	Down strokes all shaded; *t*-bar heavy; tiny hook at final stroke of letter *y*.

Instinct

A natural or acquired aptitude or tendency; a sense of what is fitting whether natural or acquired.	Disconnected letters.

Insusceptibility

Lack of susceptibility; incapacity to feel or to receive; unimpressibleness.	Vertical writing tending to the backhand.

Integrity

Uprightness of character and soundness of moral principle; honesty; probity.	Straight base line; inartistic writing; last letter in word larger than first; increasing size of letters in words; uniform writing.

Intellectuality

Quality or state of being intellectual; possession of intellectual force or endowment.	Small writing; *d*-final curved upward.

Intuition	
Quick perception of truth without conscious attention or reasoning; knowledge from within; instinctive knowledge or feeling.	Disconnected letters; ascending lines on a straight base line.
Irresolution	
Lack of resolution or firmness of purpose; want of decision.	Strokes weak; *t*-bar at left of stem.
Irritability	
The state of being irritable; susceptibility to anger or impatience.	Periods much elongated; *t*-bar at right of stem and weakly made.
Jealousy	
Any exercise of a jealous feeling; apprehensive or suspicious of being outdone; distrustful as to fidelity of another; fearful; doubtful.	Forward slope; the incurve emphasized by finals dwindling to right.
Jocosity	
Jocular; sportive; given to, done, or made, in jest.	Cross strokes scroll shape; lines ascending.
Judgment	
The mental act or attitude of decision with which the processes of observation and comparison are terminated.	Letters connected; strokes firm; style fixed; strokes and loops of one line clearly separated from lines above and below.
Judgment (Lack of)	
	Uneven writing; not well-spaced lines.
Justice (Sense of)	
Adherence to truth or fact; fairness; the quality of being just; strict uprightness; rectitude; honesty.	Lines exactly equidistant.

KEEN MINDED	
Acute; astute; calculating; clever; ardent; knowing.	Top of letters pointed; tendency to angular hand.
KINDLINESS	
Kindly disposition; the quality of being kind.	Right slope; *m* and *n* like *w* and *u;* finals never cut short.
KNAVERY	
The character or actions of one who is deceitful in dealings; roguery; dishonesty; fraud; cunning; a mean scoundrel.	Small letters *a* and *o*, tightly closed; lines irregular; small letters constantly changing in size; small letters pointed at top; finals never ascending to right.
LACK OF POISE	
Without poise; to be destitute of, without, or in want of; erratic.	Uneven, straggling hand; variable size of letters.
LANGUAGE (Command of)	
Power to obtain, use, dispose of, or control; a mastery.	Style is easy; running hand; *t* and *d* looped.
LAVISHNESS	
Spending or bestowing extravagantly, either money, speech, or actions.	Letters widely spaced.
LAZINESS	
The state or quality of being lazy; idleness; inactivity; indolence.	Round hand; writing slowly drawn.
LEVITY	
Lightness of humor or temperament; lack of mental gravity; want of seriousness or earnestness; frivolity.	Crossing of letter *t* scroll shape.
LIBERALITY	
The quality of being liberal or generous; disposition to bestow abundantly; mental broadness or comprehensiveness; freedom of opinion or utterance.	Finals long and horizontal.

LIBERAL MIND

Free from narrowness or bigotry in ideas or doctrines.

Finals long; words well spaced.

LITERARY TASTE

Versed in or devoted to literature; a liking for literary work or worthy of literature in the highest sense.

Small writing; Greek *e* and *d*.

LOGIC

The science or doctrine of correct thinking; a right use of thought or the rational powers, or the habit or gift of using them rightly; deduction; a natural and inevitable conclusion from any set of circumstances or facts.

Small writing; connected letters.

LOQUACIOUSNESS (See *Garrulous*)

Given to continual talking; talkative; chattering; one apt to disclose secrets.

Small letters *d* and *t* with wide loops; upper loop letters long; *a* and *o* open.

LOVE

Affection; to have a feeling of affection or regard for; to entertain a feeling of tenderness or passion inspired by the sexual relation.

Right slope—the more slope the greater the susceptibility; long lower loops.

LOVE OF ADMIRATION

An emotion of approbation of self; pleased or gratified contemplation of self.

Signature made with, or embellished by flourishes.

LOVE OF DISPLAY

Ostentation.

Flourishes used in writing.

LOVE OF EASE

Round hand; right slope; slow hand.

Love of Fun

The state or quality of being gay; doings prompted by spirit of light-heartedness.	*t*-crossing scroll shape with lines ascending.

Love of Luxury

	Lines widely spaced; round hand; shaded writing.

Love of the Marvelous

	Finals ascending vertically above word.

Loyalty

Loyal; hearty service in friendship, business, or love, or in any cause.	Only one form used for each letter; fine writing; straight lines.

Lucidity

To be lucid; intellectually bright and clear; mentally sound; saneness; perspicuity.	Strokes and loops of one line clearly separated from lines above and below.

Magnaminity

Generosity in sentiment or conduct toward others; loftiness of character or action; large heartedness.	Small letters high; down strokes concave; words well spaced; every letter carefully made; capitals never low; style never coarse or ungraceful; lines straight; small letters equal size.

Malice

Hate; a disposition or intent to injure another or others for the gratification of anger, jealousy, hatred, revenge, or the like.	Vertical or backhand; *p* made with the lower point sharp and upstroke on right of stem; letters never extended; *m* and *n*, unlike *w*; and *u;* no incurves.

Managerial (Manager)

Of, pertaining to, or characteristic of, a manager; one having the	Small letters neither very low nor very high; strokes and loops of one line

ability to manage; a person skilled in financial or business management.	clearly separated from lines above and below; small letters pointed at top; punctuation carefully placed; margins never wide; *t* carefully crossed; letters not widely spaced; small letters decreasing in size; unconscious, heavy shading; signature fluently written.
Masterful	
Having the characteristics or force of a master; able to control; indicative of the power, skill, or temper of a master.	Heavy, firm strokes; plain capitals; tendency to small writing; *t*-bar carefully placed across the stem; *t*-bar heavy and long.
Mathematics (Taste for)	
Liking for mathematics.	Figures well, and gracefully, formed; numerals 7 and 9 with final strokes ending gracefully below the line.
Matter of Fact Nature	
A nature comparing to absolute reality; not fanciful or imaginative.	Finals turned down.
Mechanical Tastes	
	Original method of making connections.
Mediocrity	
The quality or state of being mediocre; medium or merely commonplace ability.	Copybook style of writing; awkward or ornamental capitals.
Meditativeness	
Given to serious reflection; quiet and thoughtful disposition.	Small letters very low; *t* and *d* without loops; round hand.
Melancholy	
Morbidly gloomy; sad and downhearted; depressed in spirits; dejected.	Descending lines.

Memory	
The general capacity or function of mentally reproducing previous experiences.	Letters *i* and *j* closely dotted; *t* carefully crossed; careful punctuation.
Method	
Systematic order; regularity; orderly arrangement; system.	Every letter legible; usually small hand; neat, uniform writing, well spaced; right margin even; capitals plain.
Mildness	
Moderate in action or disposition; tender, gentle, kind; not severe or cruel.	Round, forward hand; fine writing; *t*-bar close down on stem.
Mimicry	
The act or art of imitating, especially for sport or in ridicule; simulation.	Cross strokes pointing upward.
Mind (Activity of)	
Broad mind; elegance of mind; liberal mind; scientific mind.	Small writing; letters hurriedly written some only half formed; *t*-bar on right of stem.
Minutiae	
Small or unimportant details; smallness; very exact detail.	Small letters low, but not meaning small writing; capitals small; small letters pointed at top.
Mirthfulness	
Full of mirth or merriment; merry; festive; gaiety.	Cross strokes scroll shape; lines ascending.
Miserliness	
Miserly disposition or nature; to save and hoard; avaricious.	Letters crowded together; final letters hardly finished; hooks at end of strokes; vertical or fine right slope; punctuation carefully placed.

MISTRUST

To regard with suspicion or jealousy; to suspect; doubt; lack of confidence.

Finals long and only to fill otherwise blank spaces.

MOBILITY

Characterized by ease or freedom of motion; to change easily in expression or in state of mind.

Style constantly changing; uneven writing; *t*-bar to right of stem.

MODESTY

State or quality of being modest; freedom from boldness or forwardness; unobtrusive; delicacy or purity of thought, character, feeling, or conduct.

Absence of all flourishes; inartistic writing; plain capitals.

MOODS (*See Changeableness*)

MORBIDNESS

Being in a diseased or abnormal state; not sound and healthful; denoting a diseased or unsound condition of body or mind.

Descending lines; *d* with wide loops. NOTE. Normally descending lines are not always indicative of morbidness; the descent must be unusually so, with what would appear to be "careless or indifferent" writing.

MUSCULARITY

State or quality of being muscular; one possessing well-developed muscles; powerful; vigorous.

p-stem short above, long below, looped; strokes firm.

MUSICAL

Full of music; capable of producing music, inspired with or attached to music; having a taste or talent for music.

Small letters curved at the bottom of their last down strokes; long lower loops; even swing of pen.

MUSICAL SENSUOUSNESS

The quality of being keenly susceptible to the pleasures of music through the senses and a sensuous imagination, whether of the physical or aesthetic order.

Small letters curved at the bottom of their last down strokes; even swing of the pen; cross strokes shaded particularly at the base; long lower loops.

Trait	Sign in writing
Musical Taste (Deficient)	Small letters angular or sharp at bottom of their last down strokes.
Narrow Mindedness Limited in scope; not broad or liberal in views or sentiments; bigoted.	Words close together—crowded spacing.
Neatness Strict order; cleanliness and nicety; to be neat.	Style neat; small writing—or at least not large and coarse; neat, uniform writing; well-spaced words and lines.
Negligence The act of neglecting; disregard for appearances or for conventionalities.	Punctuation entirely omitted.
Nervousness Easily disturbed or agitated owing to weak nerves; excitability; timidity; abounding in nerve or nerve-force; manifesting bodily force or vigor; exhibiting or characterized by mental force and with strong sensibilities; pertaining to a temperament characterized by a preponderance of the mental over the physical.	Angularity of the writing, while not necessarily the angular hand; strokes tremulous, characterized by the agitation that usually attends mental excitement; more generally observed in the lower and upper loop letters.
Nimble Witted Quick witted, a ready mind.	Angularity of the writing; tops of small letters pointed; base rounded.
Nobility Dignity and grace of character; not selfish, cowardly, or mean; high minded.	Small letters high; down strokes concave; words well spaced; every letter carefully made; capitals never low; style not coarse; lines straight; small letters equal size.

Notional

Existing in imagination only; visionary; not real; fantastical; ideal; given to hobbies; whimsical; fanciful; possessed of, or influenced by, pet ideas.

Lower loop letters long (must be characteristic of the writing).

Obedience

Submission to; compliance with a command or duty; the act or habit of yielding willingly to restraint.

Capitals low; *t*-bar close down on stem; strokes not firm.

Observation

The act, power, or habit of observing or taking notice; the act of perceiving or fixing the powers of sense or intellect on anything.

Connected letters; *t*-bar very short and placed squarely across the stem.

Obstinacy

Stubborn adherence to purpose, opinion, or course of action, arising from the desire to have one's own way, and generally somewhat unreasonable; stubbornness; unyielding; difficult to control or subdue.

Words connected with sweeping dashes; unconscious shading of down strokes; *f* made with stroke instead of loop; *t* heavily crossed; usually downward; finals end with hook and downward.

Oestrual (*See Erotomania*)

Being under the influence of erotic impulse; uncontrollable sexual desire.

Angularity of writing; tops of letters pointed; down strokes heavily or coarsely shaded; general appearance of writing muddy; *t* and *d* have inflated loops; lower loop letters long; tendency to ornamentation of capitals.

Opinionated

Unreasonably or stubbornly persistent in opinion; unduly attached to one's own views; conceited.

Tendency to conventional writing; connected letters—and sometimes the words; *t*-bar crossed downward —snappishly; final strokes of small letters *d* and *t* below line; hooks on final strokes.

Trait and definition	Handwriting signs
Optimism — Disposition to take the most hopeful view or to look on the brightest side of things; the belief that whatever occurs is for the best and is right and good; sanguine temperament.	Lines ascending; strong down strokes.
Orderliness — Having regard for method and arrangement; methodical; systematic.	Every letter legible; margins even; well spaced writing.
Organizer — One who has the ability to bring into systematic connection and coöperation as parts of the whole; to prepare for transaction of business; one having the ability to organize.	Usually vertical hand; tops pointed; hasty, uniform writing; lines well spaced; capitals plain; lower loop letters finish with stroke, or long loop.
Originality — The power of producing new conceptions, inventions, etc.; the quality of being novel or of having mental freshness and vigor; oddity.	Original style of letters and connections; variable size of letters (not uneven writing.)
Ostentation — The act of displaying ambitiously; display dictated by vanity.	Flourishes.
Painstaking — Taking pains; giving, or characterized by, careful attention; scrupulous and faithful in performance; diligent and accurate work.	Uniform writing; only one style used for each letter; punctuation carefully placed; well-spaced writing.
Parental Love — Love of parents.	Right slope; finals curving over to the left.

Parsimony	
Excessive saving; extreme economy; closeness; stinginess.	Letters crowded together; final letters hardly finished; hooks at end of strokes; usually in vertical hand; punctuation carefully placed.
Partiality	
Inclination to favor one side of a question more than the other; an undue bias of mind toward one party or side; unfairness; bias.	Lines unevenly spaced.
Particularization	
The act of enumerating the details or particulars of; paying attention to particulars or details.	Small letters low.
Passionate	
Capable of, or inclined to, strong passion; excitable; easily moved to anger; quick tempered.	Angularity of writing; variable size of letters; uneven writing.
Passiveness	
Being passive; inaction; passive submission in obedience or suffering; calmness, placidity.	Round hand; vertical writing, tending to right slope; the latter is more general with women.
Patience	
The quality or habit of being patient; possessing perseverance and untiring energy; ability to await events without perturbation or discontent; not in haste.	Initial strokes absent; neat, uniform writing; tendency to small writing.
Peaceableness	
Inclined to peace; not quarrelsome.	*p* made with round turn and upstroke on left of stem; round hand.
Penetration	
Ability to penetrate mentally; acuteness; sagacity; discernment; acumen.	Small letters pointed at top. Disconnected letters.

Penuriousness	
Excessively sparing or saving in the use of money; yielding little; not liberal.	Letters crowded together; final letters hardly finished; hooks at end of strokes; punctuation carefully placed.
Perception (Dullness of)	
(*See Dullness of Perception*)	Small letters rounded at top.
Perfection (Desire for)	
(*See Desire for Improvement*)	Letters mended or touched up.
Perseverance	
Act, quality, or habit of persevering; steadfast pursuit, or prosecution of a resolution; persistence in purpose and effort.	Hooks at end strokes; *y* and *g* ending in strokes instead of loops; initial strokes absent.
Persistency	
The mental quality of being persistent; obstinate resolution; tenacity; doggedness.	Hooks at end of strokes; *y* and *g* ending in strokes instead of loops; initial strokes absent.
Perspicuity	
Clearness of perception or style; the logical method of conveying an author's meaning unmistakably; freedom from obscurity, intricacy, or ambiguity; lucidity.	Small letters pointed at top; usually in small writing or smaller than medium; connected letters.
Pertinacity	
Persistent tenacity of purpose; unyielding adherence; dogged perseverance.	Words connected.
Pessimism	
A disposition to take a gloomy or despairing view of affairs; tendency to look on the dark side; a habit of anticipating failure or misfortune; depreciating good; imputing evil.	Lines descending.

Pettiness

Meanness; smallness in action or spirit; to be petty.

Small letters very low; words close together.

Petulance

Impatience; capriciousness; temporary peevishness; fretfulness.

Dots much elongated; *t*-bars at right of stem.

Philanthropy

Disposition or effort to promote the happiness or social elevation of others; comprehensive benevolence; love of man.

Letters extended; upstroke of lower loop letters turn up to right instead of to left; right slope.

Philoprogenitiveness

The love of offspring or the faculty of it; a tendency to pet or foster dependents.

Right slope; finals curling over to left.

Physical Activity

Lower loop letters made with stroke and long; angularity of writing; strokes firm.

Physical Inactivity

Lower loop letters short below and longer above.

Physical Weakness

(Not illness)

p-stem long above and short below.

Pleasure (Desire for)

Lines more ascending than the words.

Poetic Taste

Disconnected letters; long *f* loops; *w* rounded, emphasized by a lasso stroke.

Poise	
The state or quality of being balanced; equilibrium; rest.	Round hand; *a* and *o* closed; small to medium sized writing.
Positiveness	
Openly and plainly expressed; explicit; not admitting of doubt or denial; incontestible; free from doubt or hesitation.	Angular writing; heavy strokes; *t*-bar heavy and club shaped; lower stroke of *p* pointed and turned up on right of stroke.
Practicality	
The quality of being practical; one said to be trained by, or in, practice or experience; opposed to ideal.	Margins absent, tending to angular, vertical writing; neat, uniform, well-spaced writing; lines straight; connected letters; *f* stroke instead of loop.
Precipitousness	
Headlong in disposition or hasty in action; rashness; the act of urging a matter forward prematurely or inconsiderately.	*t*-cross dashed off to right of, and above, stem.
Precision	
To be precise; the quality of style that expresses exactly and clearly what a writer or speaker intends.	Neat, uniform writing, every letter carefully made; *t* carefully crossed; punctuation carefully placed; the tendency is to small writing, or less than medium.
Presumption	
Blind, headstrong, or over-weening confidence or self-assertion; venturesomeness in undertaking something without reasonable prospect of success, or against the usual probabilities of safety; the act of forming a judgment on probable grounds; assuming too much.	Strokes firm; capitals too high; usually in the vertical hand, and larger than medium in size.

Pretension

A claim assumed or advanced, whether false or well-founded as to possession, right, dignity; to pretend.

Capitals too high; flourishes.

Prevarication

The act of provoking an action or a quibble or misleading statement, intended to deceive, or a seeming denial or affirmation that is not express falsehood.

Letters in each word are decreased in size—the last letter being smaller than the first letter in the word.

Pride

Unreasonable conceit of one's own superiority, whether as to talent, wealth, beauty, accomplishments, rank, office, or other distinction, with correspondingly contemptuous feeling towards others; a proper sense of dignity, character, and worth; aversion to that which is or is to be unworthy of one's character, station, or name; self-respect.

Capitals too high for body of writing; small letter *d* with high stem, either looped or sharply made.

Procrastination

Putting off; dilatoriness; delay, especially culpable delay.

Uneven writing; *t*-cross at left of stem; *i*-dot to left and high.

Prodigality

Extravagance in the expenditure of money or things; vicious or unnecessary expenditure.

Letters widely spaced; lower loop letters extend to line below.

Progressiveness

Advancement; making or tending to progress.

Words well spaced; heavy unconscious shading; *t* heavily crossed.

Protectiveness	
The desire to shield from harm or intrusion.	Finals curling over to left.
Prudence	
Carefulness to avoid practical mistakes; caution; good judgment and foresight in practical affairs; economy; discretion.	Style of writing fixed; punctuation carefully placed; *t*-bar never at right of stem.
Psychic Qualities	
Of or pertaining to unusual operations of the mind or to occult phenomena.	Disconnected letters—the more the letters are separated the greater the significance; fine writing; well-spaced writing; lines widely spaced.
Pugnacious	
Disposed or inclined to fight; quarrelsome; contentious.	Heavy, coarse writing; letters begin with a straight inflexible stroke; letters never compressed; *t*-bar at right of and above stem; *p* made with lower point sharp and upstroke at right of stem.
Punctuality	
Being punctual in any sense; promptness in doing, or exactness in occurring; faithfulness to a time promised.	*t*-bar never at left of stem; punctuation carefully placed.
Purity	
Character or state of being pure in any sense; moral cleanness; innocence.	Down strokes light.
Quarrelsomeness	
Given to quarreling; apt or disposed to quarrel; irascibleness; a contentious disposition.	Disconnected letters; *t*-bar higher than top of stem and to the right; *p* made with lower point sharp and upstroke at right of stem; initial strokes absent; *i*-dots much elongated; capitals never low; letters never compressed.

Quickness	
State or quality of being quick; liveliness; activity; readiness; acuteness of perception or sensibility; alertness.	Angular writing; hasty and indistinct writing; *i*-dot at right and high; *t*-bar at right of stem.
Quietness	
The state or quality of being quiet in any sense.	Vertical hand; round writing; fine writing; tops of small letters never pointed.
Rapacity	
The quality or character of being rapacious; the practice or act of obtaining profit by oppression; avarice.	Letters crowded together; final letters hardly finished; hooks at end of strokes; uneven writing; tendency to the angular, vertical hand; punctuation carefully placed.
Rashness	
The quality or state of being rash; recklessness.	Finals ascending to right; punctuation carelessly done.
Reasoning Powers (Deductive)	
The mental act, process, or faculty of deriving conclusions from facts or propositions admitted or assumed for the sake of argument.	Letters connected.
Recklessness	
Rashness; destitude of heed or concern for consequences; heedless of danger; desperate; not caring or noting; neglect.	Finals ascending to right; punctuation carelessly done.
Refinement	
Fineness or chasteness of thought, taste, manner, or language; freedom from coarseness or vulgarity.	Style graceful and cultivated.

Reflectiveness	
Given to reflection or thought; meditative; turning the attention upon the processes of the mind itself.	Small writing; *t* and *d* without loops.
Reliability	
The quality of being reliable; that which may be relied upon; worthy of confidence; to be depended upon; trustworthiness; honesty.	Lines straight; small letters equal size.
Reserve	
To keep back; to keep one's own thoughts; reserve of manner; to be distant, undemonstrative.	Letters compressed; *a* and *o* closed.
Resistence	
The means or power of resisting; to make opposition; antagonize.	Cross strokes strong.
Resolution	
The state or character of being resolute; steadfastness of purpose and firmness in adhering to it; active fortitude; determination.	Strokes becoming heavier toward end.
Responsiveness	
Inclined or ready to respond; being in accord, sympathy, or harmony; susceptibility.	Forward hand, very sloping.
Restless	
Always active or moving; never quiet; unable or disinclined to rest; given to incessant activity; uneasy; constantly seeking change.	Style of writing constantly changing; letters hurriedly written, some only half formed.
Restrained Buoyancy (*See Buoyancy Restrained*)	

Reticence	
The quality of being reticent; reserve in speech.	Letters compressed; *a* and *o* closed.
Revengeful	
Cherishing the disposition and purpose of revenge; vindictive.	Heavy writing.
Reverence	
Veneration; regarding with profound respect and affection; treating with deference.	Right slope; capitals low; down strokes light.
Rhythm (Sense of)	
Harmonious movement or sound; accent, tune; characterized by regular recurrence of impulse.	Letters extended; even swing of pen.
Righteous	
Characterized by the endeavor to conform to the right; upright.	Straight lines.
Romanticness	
State of being romantic; extravagantly ideal; sentimental rather than rational; fancifulness; visionary; dreamy.	Exclamation, interrogation, quotation marks, and underscore much used; long loops.
Sadness	
The state or condition of being sad; depression of spirits; a feeling of grief or gloom.	Lines descending.
Sagacity	
The quality of being sagacious; shrewdness; ready and accurate discernment and judgment.	Small letters pointed at top; some letters in words disconnected; strokes and loops of one line clearly separated from lines above and below; style fixed.

Sarcasm	
A keenly ironical, scornful, or taunting expression; cutting and reproachful language.	Small letters *d* and *t* with sharply pointed stems.
Scientific Mind	
A mind capable of understanding scientific subjects; having exact knowledge or perception; well-versed in science or a science.	Letters square shaped.
Secretiveness	
Inclination or tendency to secrete or conceal, the faculty and disposition that induces concealment or deception.	Crowded writing; letters *a* and *o* tightly closed; final of small letter *s* tied to the up-stroke in a little "twist."
Self-Appreciation	
Appreciation of one's self; undue consciousness; self-respect.	Capitals high.
Self-Assertion	
The characteristic of asserting one's self or one's rights or claims in an assuming manner.	Capitals too high; strokes firm; letters never compressed.
Self-Assurance	
The mental state of feeling confident of one's own abilities.	Finals ascending to right; *p* made with lower point sharp and upstroke on right of stem; lines straight; capitals never low; letters never compressed; strokes firm; style fixed.
Self-Consciousness	
The act, condition, or quality of being or becoming immediately aware of the activities or states of self; reflexively conscious.	Capitals high; finals descending to right; usually in backhand writing.

Self-Control

The act, power, or habit of having one's faculties or energies, especially the inclinations and emotions, under control; self-command.

Strokes firm; *t*-bar not at left of stem; *i*-dots round.

Self-Esteem

Self-respect; a good opinion of one's self or of one's character, attainments, or powers; the faculty that gives dignity and self reliance.

Capitals high.

Self-Interest

One's own interest or advantage, especially without regard to what is right or due to others.

Backhand writing.

Selfishness

Undue regard for one's own interest, gratification, advantage, or the like, regardless of others.

Finals absent; large, heavy, diffuse writing.

Self-Reliant

Relying on one's own abilities, resources, or judgment; independence of character.

Tops of small letters pointed; more generally in the angular hand.

Self-Respect

Respect or proper regard for one's own person and character.

Capitals high; *d*-stem high; *a* and *o* open.

Self-Restraint

The act or process of restraining; holding one's self back, as of the passions, or by the force of one's own will; mental, moral, or physical hindrance; repression.

Round, forward hand; words close together; strokes and loops of one line clearly separated from lines above and below.

Trait	Indication
Self-Satisfaction	
Satisfaction with one's own actions and characteristics; self-complacency.	Last stroke of capital *M* higher than the first or second stroke.
Self-Sufficiency	
Overweening confidence in one's own endowments, knowledge, or worth; self-satisfied; haughty; overbearing; self-conceited.	Last stroke of capital *M* higher than the first or second strokes.
Sense of Form (*See Form*)	
	Capitals simple, graceful, and print-like.
Sense of Justice (*See Justice*)	
	Lines exactly equidistant.
Sensibility	
State or quality of being sensible; the power or capacity of feeling, including both sensation and aesthetic and rational emotion; susceptibility to outside influences.	Right slope—very sloping.
Sensitiveness	
The state or quality of being sensitive; impressionable.	Letters incurve; *d* looped; variable size of letters.
Sensuality	
Sensual; free indulgence in carnal or sensual pleasure, or in any mode of it; the spirit that cherishes the animal appetites and seeks their gratification.	Coarse heavy hand; usually in large hand; down strokes muddy.
Sensuousness	
The state of being keenly susceptible to influences through the senses and sensuous imagination, whether of the physical or aesthetic order; opposed to spiritual.	Cross strokes shaded.

Sensuousness (Absence of)

Not sensuous.	Cross strokes light; fine writing.

Sensuousness of Color

Keenly fond of, or moved to, ecstacy by color.	Cross strokes shaded; capitals are simple, graceful, and curved.

Sensuousness of Form

Sense of configuration; appreciation and recognition of shapes, outlines, and contours.	Cross strokes shaded; capitals are simple, graceful, and print like.

Sensuousness (Musical)

Love of melody; musical ability; sense of tone; the ability to appreciate concord, modulation, and harmony.	Cross strokes shaded; small letters curved at bottom of their last down strokes; lower loops long; even swing of pen.

Sentimentality

State of being sentimental; over indulgence in sentimental feeling.	Round, forward slope; exclamation, interrogation, quotation marks, and underscore much used.

Sequence of Thought

Deduction.	Letters connected.

Seriousness

Grave and earnest in quality, manner, feeling, or disposition; not inclined to joke or trifle; thoughtful, sober, earnest.	Cross strokes straight.

Servility

Abject or cringing submission or deference; slavishness; to be servile.	Capitals excessively low; signature smaller than body of text.

Severity

Sternness; the quality of being severe; harshness or cruelty of disposition or treatment; want of kindness or gentleness in dealing with others.	Vertical, tending to the backhand; angularity of the writing; strokes firm; style fixed; *m* and *n* unlike the *w* and *u;* letters not extended; punctuation not carelessly done.

Shallowness

Narrow mindedness; lacking intellectual depth; not wise or profound; superficial.	Words close together; *t*-crossings weak.

Shrewd

Having keen insight, especially in small or worldly matters; displaying keen discernment; sharp; sagacious.	Small letters pointed at top; some letters disconnected; strokes and loops of one line clearly separated from lines above and below; style fixed.

Shyness

Keeping away through sensitiveness; inclined to shrink back from bashfulness; reserve; coyness.	Letters compressed; no flourishes; capitals low; cross strokes straight.

Simplicity of Taste

Tastes that are simple; absence of ostentation; free from affectation or pretension.	Capitals made by enlarging small letters; vertical hand; fine writing; inartistic formation and variable size of letters.

Sincerity

State or quality of being sincere; honesty of purpose or character; freedom from hypocrisy, deceit or simulation; truthfulness; honesty.	Lines straight; small letters equal size; inartistic, schoolboy hand, or the tendency to ungraceful writing; letters increase in size in the words.

Skepticism

A doubting or incredulous state of mind; requiring more proof; distrustful.	Capitals narrow at base; connected letters.

Sleepiness

Inclination to sleep; drowsiness.	Words running into mere wandering lines.

Slovenliness

The state or quality of being slovenly; carelessness in one's dress, or neglect of cleanliness; negligent of neatness and order.	General style slovenly; diffused writing; uneven, straggling hand; left margins uneven; punctuation carelessly done.

Slowness	
Quality of being slow in any sense.	In cultured hand—the vertical; in illiterate hand—the forward slope; *t*-bars to left of stem; *i*-dot to left.
Slyness	
Quality of being sly; craftiness; cunning.	*a* and *o* tightly closed, lines irregular, small letters constantly varying in size; small letters pointed at top; finals never ascending to right.
Sociability	
The quality or character of being sociable; amiability.	Diffused writing; *m* and *n* like *w* and *u;* letters extended; capitals not too high; style not eccentric; down stroke of *p* rounding up to left rather than pointed to right.
Social Ambition	
Disposition; to hold friendly intercourse with others; companionable; sociable.	First strokes of capital *N* or *M* much higher than second or third.
Speculative	
Given to speculation; using the discursive method of intellect, resulting from inference, as opposed to intuition and experience; the analytical and inferential intellect.	Writing that is not well spaced; lower loop letters extend into line below.
Speech (Fluency of)	
Command of language; the faculty of expressing thought fluently and readily.	Easy running hand; *d* and *t* looped.
Spirituality	
The character of being spiritual or free from worldliness; the faculty that gives a feeling of confidence; sense of the spiritual; opposed to materiality.	All down strokes light—no shade; disconnected letters very marked; plain capitals.

Stability

The quality or character of being steady or constant; steadfastness of resolution or purpose; constancy.

Style of writing fixed; all down strokes are of the same slant.

Steadiness

The quality of being steady; free from intemperance and dissipation; industrious, sober, reliable; constant in mind or conduct.

Style of writing fixed; all down strokes lightly made and of the same slant.

Sternness

The quality of being stern; having an austere disposition; unyielding in character; rigidly steadfast; unmoved by sympathy or emotions; resolute.

Vertical writing, with tendencies to the backhand; strokes firm; style fixed; letters not extended; punctuation not carelessly placed.

Stinginess

The quality of being stingy; close and penurious; avarice.

Letters crowded together; final letters hardly finished; hooks at end of strokes; if in cultured hand the punctuation is carefully placed; if in large hand strokes are coarse; if in small hand the strokes are fine.

Straightforwardness

Frank, honest, open; proceeding in a direct manner; undeviating; free from prevarication or concealment.

Straight lines—the lines should be straight across the page and the words also straight on the line; *a* and *o* open.

Strength

Muscularity; the quality or condition of being physically strong; mental or moral force; effectiveness, or power of endurance: binding or conclusive force, as strength of will.

Small letter *p* made with the stem short above and long below, in either loop or stroke, the longer the lower stroke the greater the signification.

Struggle Against Depression	
To put forth great effort to overcome or resist oppression or morbid feelings; a succession of efforts to overcome the lowering of the vital powers.	Words that cant downward on the descending lines more than the lines themselves.
Struggle Between Heart and Head	
An effort to decide between the dictates of the mental forces and the sympathies.	Loop letters at different angles.
Stubbornness	
Inflexible in opinion or intention; not to be moved or persuaded by reason; unyielding in character.	Many successive words connected.
Suavity	
The state or quality of being suave; agreeable smoothness of manner; blandness; urbanity; the faculty that gives urbanity and a smooth easiness in speech and conduct; tact.	First letter of a word larger than the rest.
Submissiveness	
The quality of being submissive; yielding; obedient; docile; willing or inclined to submit; humbleness.	Capitals low; *t*-bar close down on the stem; strokes not very firm.
Susceptibility	
The state or quality of being susceptible to influences or of easily receiving impressions; the ability to receive or be impressed by deep emotions or strong feelings.	Writing that is very sloping to the right.

Suspicion

The act of suspecting; conjecture, with little or no evidence to support it, that something wrong exists or is going to happen; unreasonable imagination or apprehension; mistrust; doubt.

Finals long only to fill otherwise blank spaces; tendency to small writing; crowded writing; descending lines.

Sympathy

A feeling of compassion for another's sufferings or evils; pity; an agreement of affections or inclinations or natural temperament, which makes persons agreeable to one another.

Right slope; the incurve; letters extended; finals never cut short.

System

Orderly combination or arrangement; the state or quality of being orderly.

Every letter legible; neat uniform writing; well spaced writing; left margins even down the page.

Taciturnity

Disinclination to talk; habitual silence or reserve.

Letters *d* and *t*-with pointed stem; upstrokes of these letters at left of stem; *a* and *o* closed.

Tact

A quick or intuitive appreciation of what is fit, proper, or right; fine or ready mental discernment shown in saying or doing the proper thing, especially in avoiding what would offend or disturb.

First letter of word larger than rest of word; small writing or at least smaller than medium; neat, uniform writing; *a* and *o* closed.

Talkativeness

Given to much talking, especially idle talk; loquaciousness; communicativeness.

Small letters *d* and *t* with loops; small letters *b* and *t* with small initial hooks; *a* and *o* open.

Tardiness Slow movement, gait, or pace; not coming at the appointed or expected time; dilatoriness; procrastination.	*t*-bar at left of stem. *i* and *j* frequently undotted.
Taste (Architectural) Liking for constructive or architectural pursuits.	Simple, graceful, and print-like capitals.
Taste (Artistic) Liking for the arts—music, poetry; aesthetic.	Long loops to lower loop letters; disconnected letters; simple and graceful capitals.
Taste (for Color) Love for and perception of, color; sense of shades, tints, hues, and blending colors with taste and discrimination.	Simple, graceful, and curved capitals.
Taste (for Designing) Sense of configuration; appreciation for, and recognition of, shape, outlines and contours.	Simple, graceful and print-like capitals.
Taste (for Mathematics) Mental arithmetic; faculty for computing numerically; mathematical talent.	Figures well and easily formed, all attempt at ornamentation of figures absent; careful and precise style of writing.
Taste for Music (Deficient) Lack of melody; no musical ability; no sense of tune; inability to appreciate concord, modulation, and harmony.	Small letters angular at bottom of their last down strokes.

TASTE (Literary)

Literary discrimination; the ability to write; literary accomplishment; cultured; fondness or liking for literary pursuits.	Hasty writing; smaller than medium; variable size of letters; Greek *d;* Greek *e;* correct punctuation; in larger hand than medium, the characters are variable in size, hastily written, diffused and unevenly spaced on the page; very plain capitals in cultured hand only.

TASTE (Mechanical)

Constructive talents.	Original methods of making connections.

TASTE (Poetic)

A liking for poetry and aesthetics.	Small letter *w* rounded, emphasized by the "lasso" stroke; long lower loop letters.

TASTE (Simplicity of)

Simple tastes.	Capitals made by enlarging small letters.

TEACHABLENESS

Capable of being, and willing to be, taught; an aptness for learning; docility.	Words not connected; cross strokes never pointing downward; capitals never too high; words well spaced.

TELEGRAPHER'S HAND

Style of writing acquired by telegraph operators after long practice at "receiving."	Words connected by festoon-like lines.

TEMPER

Heat of mind or passion; angry excitement; disposition to become angry.	Usually in the angular hand, either slope; *t*-bar above stem, often flying off stem to the right.

TENACITY

Tenaciousness; firmness or persistency, as of purpose; retentiveness of memory.	Angular writing; hooks at end of final strokes.

Tenderness	
The quality of being tender or merciful in any sense.	The right slope.
Thievishness	
Addicted to the practice of theft; given to stealing; partaking of the nature of theft, as a thievish advantage.	Small letters constantly varying in size; letters close together; writing never extended; lines irregular; lines irregularly spaced; hooks at end of final strokes; base line wavy; small letters *a* and *o* tightly closed.
Thoroughness	
Completeness; the quality of being thorough, marked by careful attention throughout; leaving nothing undone.	Tendency to small writing; small letters low; punctuation carefully placed.
Thoughtfulness	
State of being thoughtful; mindful; attentive; careful; full of, busied with, or given to, thought; meditation; contemplative.	Punctuation carefully placed.
Thoughtlessness	
Manifesting lack of thought or care; lacking ability to think; dullness.	Diffused writing; punctuation carelessly placed; small letters *a* and *o* open.
Thrift	
Care and prudence in the management of one's resources; economy; frugality.	Letters close together; no margins; punctuation carefully placed; neat, uniform writing.
Tidiness	
Neatness and order; cleanliness; proper arrangement; free from any sign of neglect; orderly disposition or habit.	Neat writing; lines well spaced; *t*-bar carefully placed across stem.

Time	
To adapt to the time or the occasion. The ability to comprehend the laws of time; to understand metre and rhythm, as in music and harmony.	Easy swing of pen; letters extended.
Timidity	
Want of courage or boldness to face danger or publicity; timorousness; fearfulness.	Finals descending to right.
Tranquillity	
The quality of being tranquil; freedom from, or superior to, all disturbing influences; calmness.	*i*-dots and periods round.
Trickery	
Artifice; stratagem; deception; cheating; cunning.	Lines irregular; small letters constantly varying in size and pointed at top; finals never ascending; *a* and *o* closed.
Triviality	
The state or quality of being trivial; interested in trifles; low, petty ability or wit; pettiness; unscholarly.	Words close together; small letters very low (not meaning small writing.)
Trust	
A confident reliance of the mind on the integrity, veracity, justice, or other sound principle of another person.	Finals not used to fill otherwise blank spaces.
Trustworthy	
That may be depended upon; worthy of confidence; reliable.	Straight lines; simple unpretentious writing.

Truthfulness	
Habitually speaking the truth; veracious; reliable; accurate; candidness; honesty.	Lines straight; small letters equal size; increasing size of letters, the last letter being larger than the first; *a* and *o* open.
Tune	
Order; right mood; to adapt to or put in accord with; in harmony with.	Small letters curved at the bottom of their last down strokes in each word; long loops.
Unambitious Nature	
Without ambition.	Cross strokes descending; *t*-crossing weakly done.
Unassuming	
Making no assumption of personal superiority or worth; making no pretentions; modest; humble.	Fine writing; no shading; plain, simple formation of letters without regard for appearances; well-spaced lines.
Unbalanced	
Not in a state of equipoise or equilibrium; lacking mental balance; unsteady; unsound; erratic.	Uneven writing; lines irregularly spaced; third or last stroke of capital *M* higher than the first stroke; diffused hand, words straggling or spread over the line; *a* and *o* open.
Unimaginative Nature	
Limited in the powers of imagination.	Upper strokes of letters short; *t*-bar never above stem.
Unobservant Nature	
The faculty of observing not developed or strong.	*t*-bar very long.
Untruthfulness	
The quality or character of being untruthful; want of veracity; deceitfulness.	Lines irregular; small letters constantly varying in size; *a* and *o* tightly closed; small letter *s* closed or tied to upstroke.

Uprightness	
The quality or state of being upright; morally correct, just, and honest; adhering to rectitude.	Plain, simple writing without flourish; *a* and *o* open; *t*-bar across stem; *d* with high stem.
Urbanity	
Refined or elegant courtesy; suavity; politeness; amiability.	Letters extended; capitals not too high; style not eccentric; *m* and *n* like *w* and *u;* down strokes of *p* rounding up to left rather than pointed to right.
Vacillation	
Fluctuation of mind; changeableness.	Style constantly changing; uneven writing; straggling hand; variable size of letters.
Vanity	
To be vain; a feeling of shallow pride, manifested in a small way and on slight grounds; inordinate self-esteem, conceit.	Capitals too high; flourishes; words close together.
Veneration	
The feeling of one who looks upon or treats with honor the deference due to something noble, dignified, or sacred, especially age or rank.	Right slope; capitals low; down strokes light; fine writing; no shading.
Versatility	
The character or faculty of turning with ease from one occupation or task to another.	Finals concave; variable size of letters; horizontal lines; plain capitals.
Violence	
The quality, character, or state of being violent, either in a physical or moral sense.	Small letters constantly varying in size; ungraceful style of writing; letters never extended; no incurves; capitals ungraceful and coarse; down strokes muddy.

Virility

The state, quality, or character of being virile; manliness; quality or action.	Normal, steady hand; down strokes shaded and firm; lower loop letters long; *p* long below and short above.

Vivacity

Vivaciousness; liveliness; sprightliness of temper or behavior.	Letters hurriedly written, some only half formed; small letters *t* and *d* looped; letters extended; *m* and *n* like *w, u;* angularity of writing.

Volubility

Readiness or fluency in speech.	Upper loop letters long; *d* and *t* with wide loops.

Voluptuousness

The state or quality of being voluptuous; sensual gratification; indulgence in pleasures or luxuries—sensuous ones.	Writing slowly drawn out; down strokes muddy.

Vulgarity

Low condition in life; commonness; lack of refinement in conduct or speech.	Capitals complicated and ungraceful.

Want of Dignity

Lacking in dignity.	Down strokes convex.

Wastefulness

Expending or using lavishly or prodigally; extravagance.	Letters widely spaced; wide margins.

Watchfulness

Full of care or vigilance; careful to observe; cautious.	Dashes in place of periods or the occasional use of dashes for periods.

Weak Will

Not having strong will power.	Strokes weak, variable size of letters; *t*-bar weakly crossing the stem or to left of it.

Will Power

The power of controlling one's own movements and internal states, feelings, and thoughts by conscious, deliberate choice; the faculty of self-determination; directive effort; strong determination; practical enthusiasm; energy of character.

Writing that is straight on the page; ascending lines that are straight; down strokes that are shaded (unconsciously shaded); *t*-bar firm and crossing the stem or carefully and deliberately across the stem, or pointing upward across the stem, or heavily dashed to right of stem, generally in vertical writing.

Willfulness

A spirit of unyielding determination; stubbornness; self-will; tendency to wildness; waywardness.

Shaded writing, usually unconscious; final stroke of small letter *d* below line; final stroke of small letter *t* below line.

Wit

Humor; keen, sudden, brief perception of the incongruous or ludicrous.

Finals turned up; letters hurriedly written and only half formed; usually in the diffused hand; *t*-bar made scroll shape.

Worry

State of perplexing care, anxiety, or annoyance; vexation; fretfulness.

Lines that descend with words more descending than the lines; *i* dots made of elongated dashes, short and weakly struck; punctuation carefully placed.

Yielding Nature

The act of one whose nature is yielding. Acquiescence or complaisance; surrender.

Strokes weak; no hooks at end of strokes.

Zeal

Passionate ardor for a cause or, less often, intense eagerness; enthusiastic devotion; fervor.

Upper strokes long; writing energetic; dashes never used for periods; down strokes shaded.